Theses on the Article of

Justification

as Taught in Holy Scripture and the Confessions of Christ's Holy Church with Special Attention to "Objective Justification"

as discussed during the 2013 Colloquium and Synod of the

Evangelical Lutheran Diocese of North America

and later approved in the following form
by the pastors of the diocese

and

The Forensic Appeal to the Throne of Grace in the Theology of the Lutheran Age of Orthodoxy:

A Reflection on Atonement and Its Relationship to Justification

by Rev. Paul A. Rydecki

Repristination Press
Malone, Texas

Published in 2014

REPRISTINATION PRESS
P.O Box 173
Bynum, Texas 76631

REPRISTINATIONPRESS.COM

ISBN 1-891469-54-1

Table of Contents

Theses on the Article of Justification as Taught in Holy Scripture and the Confessions of Christ's Holy Church with Special Attention to "Objective Justification"

as discussed during the 2013 Colloquium and Synod of the Evangelical Lutheran Diocese of North America and later approved in the following form by the pastors of the diocese

Preface

A pastor was recently removed from a church body's clergy roster, ostensibly for false doctrine concerning the Article of Justification. His statements concerning this article of doctrine were entirely compatible with the fathers of Lutheran orthodoxy,[1] but were considered "inadequate," because they did not fully express certain formulations demanded by said church body. The official position of the (defunct) Evangelical Lutheran Synodical Conference of North America (and of the current bodies that were constituent of it) is clear from, e.g, the 1932

1 By this phrase, we are restricting our present consideration to the period beginning with Martin Luther and ending with Johann Gerhard (c. AD 1515–1637).

"Brief Statement of the Doctrinal Position of the Missouri Synod," to wit, the teaching of "Objective Justification." However, that teaching[2] has by no means been consistent throughout the publications or seminaries of said bodies since that time. The following theses examine both the terminology and the teaching of "Objective Justification" to see whether it was what was understood by the old Lutheran dogmaticians and exegetes, complementary to what they taught concerning the Article of Justification, or inimical to it.

First, A Matter of Definition:

"Objective Justification" has been variously presented

- as merely a synonym for unlimited atonement,
- as properly referring to justification as the object of faith,
- and as the 'proper' understanding of the teaching.[3]

This last view states that it is a fact[4] that Mankind has been not only atoned for by Christ, but actually declared free from sin by God prior to faith. In the resurrection, it is said, God actually absolved the world.[5] Indeed,

2 Or even what is meant by that term.

3 I.e., as found in, e.g., Pieper's *Christian Dogmatics* and the Missouri Synod's *Brief Statement.*

4 Whether believed or not; thus, "objective."

5 Note, that among LCMS theologians it is not generally stated as "all men," but as "Mankind" or "the world," so that the 'class' is absolved, but no persons in particular. Among the WELS theologians, this distinction doesn't seem to be maintained. Cf. "This We Believe," IV:1, http://www.wels.net/what-we-believe/statements-beliefs/this-we-believe/justification; Dr. Siegbert Becker's 1982 essay, "Objective Justification," p. 1,14, http://www.wlsessays.net/files/BeckerJustification.*pdf*; Forrest Bivens's essay, "Getting The Right Message Out—And Getting It Out The Right Way," in the section where he abuses Romans 3:23–24, http://www.wlsessays.net/files/BivensMessage.*pdf*; John Schaller in his *The Wauwatosa Theology,* Volume 1, p. 459,

Pieper says[6] that if this idea is not maintained Christianity is completely lost and the Gospel is necessarily turned into a set of rules by which to gain God's favor.

To be clear, then, in these theses, we will mean by the term "Objective Justification" precisely and solely what was taught by Pieper in his *Dogmatics,* which is what is the stated official position of the LCMS in its *Brief Statement,* to wit: "Objective Justification" is the dogmatic assertion that a forensic declaration was made by God in the resurrection (because of a change in His heart effected by the atoning death of the Christ) that Man is without sin.

Such a teaching, it is stated, requires a 'second part' for justification to be enjoyed by any person: that he personally and individually receive what God has objectively declared of all *together.* While in practice we have often witnessed a minimizing of the Means of Grace in bodies that hold to this teaching, that is certainly not the intent of those who first promoted it, since such reception is done by means of faith that is created in the one receiving by the Holy Ghost's use of the Gospel.[7]

Thus, we are brought to assert the following:

466–467; and David Kuske in his comments on 2 Corinthians 5:19 in "Making Use of Our Lutheran Heritage—'Objective Justification' in Our Mission Outreach Based on an Exegesis of 2 Corinthians 5:18–19," p. 7,9,11, http://www.wlsessays.net/files/KuskeOutreach.*pdf*.

6 *Christian Dogmatics,* II, 347–351.

7 Thus, one sees C.F.W. Walther, for example, rightly promoting the use of the Gospel in all its forms (i.e., that which is read, preached upon, spoken directly in Holy Absolution, or tied to physical elements in Holy Baptism and the Lord's Supper, the Means [or Channels] of Salvation, as they are properly called) to distribute and confer what God the Son has won by His passive and active obedience, for which purpose Christ instituted the Office of the Holy Ministry.

Thesis 1

It is our unanimous understanding that the Christ paid for and made full satisfaction for every sin of every person ever to enter this world. The teaching of any sort of "limited atonement" is, therefore, condemned, as is any notion that would make Christ's atonement less than sufficient, such as an idea that an individual's salvation is in any way dependent upon himself (whether with regard to character, works, disposition, or any other thing that might be attributed to Man). In spite of the rhetoric of some, we contend that both those who hold to and those who reject a Synodical Conference understanding of "Objective Justification" are in agreement on this Thesis.

Thesis 2

It is our unanimous understanding that salvation is received by the individual sinner only through faith, that none are to be regarded as saved except through faith, and that faith is (in keeping with the previous Thesis) not a work of Man, but a gift from God, given through His appointed Means of Gospel and Sacrament. We further hold that the Gospel is not mere information, but that which actually confers what it announces or promises. Further, we grant that those who oppose the teaching of these theses by adherence to the Waltherian[8] formulation of "Objective Justification" will consider our words thus far to be in agreement with their own.

We condemn every form of universalism and any thought that Man has the merit and righteousness of

---

8 Cf., e.g., C.F.W. Walther, *Justification: Subjective and Objective,* translated by Kurt E. Marquart, Fort Wayne, Indiana: Concordia Theological Seminary Press, 1982.

Christ applied to him other than through that faith which is created by these *media salutis.*

Thesis 3

The Calvinist doctrine that God desires only some to be saved is entirely rejected by us as contrary to God's Word as clearly set forth in the Lutheran Confessions. So is the Huberian[9] thought that God has actually elected all to salvation but some, somehow, fall away by failing to grasp the "Objective Justification" made at the cross and pronounced in the resurrection. Nor is any sort of Arminianism (including any Arminian-shaded concept of election *intuitu fidei*) to be received. Rather, we contend, both those who teach Waltherian "Objective Justification" and those who teach that Walther's position is contrary to the Reformers' understanding of the Article of Justification confess, instead (with the Book of Concord), that God has elected only in connection with Christ. Further, we confess that in such election He has both foreseen and caused to be all things needed to bring men to faith and to keep them therein (i.e., the sending of God the Son and God the Holy Ghost, the establishment of the Sacraments, the Office of the Ministry, and so forth).

---

9 Samuel Huber (1547–1624), a former Calvinist, was brought to Wittenberg as a professor after making a good defense against the Calvinists at Tübingen, but within three years they discovered that he was straying from the outline of Justification in common use by Lutherans, using novel terminology and accusing his fellow professors of Calvinism when they rejected his new teaching: "Our Churches have always taught and still teach the justification that is by faith and that pertains to believers, but that by no means extends to the whole world." (Hunnius, *A Clear Explanation of the Controversy among the Wittenberg Theologians Concerning Regeneration and Election,* p. 57; see, also, the next four pages of this work for a summary of the full course Huber's errors)

Thesis 4

As the above theses would not have been agreed upon by all parties in previous controversies over the Article of Justification, historical battles over aspects of this article are well brought into the picture, but none of them completely speaks to the current discussion, whether the Wittenberg faculty's dealings with Huber or the Synodical Conference's fear of an encroaching Arminianism/Semi-Pelagianism during the controversy regarding predestination. It is unfitting simply to label one another as having a position identical to one in a previous battle,[10] though it may rightly be said that a position bears similarities or could lead to such a historic position.[11] That is, we must not condemn by the application of labels, but must address what is actually taught or not taught by any party.

Thesis 5

At the same time, our avoidance of such anachronism must not render what has been said in previous controversies inapplicable: that which has been resoundingly condemned or refuted in one controversy is no less condemned and refuted when a new controversy comes upon us. While new controversies continue to arise (i.e., Satan continues to refine his troubling of the Church), we must refine and extend what has been confirmed in the past, not contradict and destroy it.

As we read in the first Article of the Formula of Concord, "As regards terms and expressions, it is best and safest to use and retain the form of sound words employed

10 Unless one can absolutely show such to be the case.
11 If and only if it can be demonstrated that such is so.

concerning this [or any] article in the Holy Scriptures and the above-mentioned books," (i.e., the other accepted confessional documents; Thorough Declaration I:50) we must not 'refine' any article of doctrine in any way that contradicts that "form of sound words." One cannot correct a supposed insufficiency by contradiction; to do so, it must be admitted, is to set aside and reject the previous teaching.

Thesis 6

It is to be remembered, too, that the private writings of the fathers do not establish an article of doctrine or have the authority to define things contrary to Scripture and the Confessions. Citing a father—or the greatest number of fathers—does not automatically win the argument on that basis. Nonetheless, when we hear the testimony of those of the era immediately following the Reformation, we rightly assume that they are more certain of what those writing, compiling, and teaching the Lutheran Symbols were asserting than those of later ages would be; that is, the presumption of accuracy is with those closest to the era or controversy unless and until proven otherwise.

To the possible contention that those who come later may see things in a clearer light by means of those who came before, we respond that we are not discussing whether we might find a better way to present an article of doctrine than our fathers did, but simply ascertaining what they actually taught. We may certainly find things to say, e.g., about the Baptism of infants that are not said in the Large Catechism, but the Catechism tells us what Luther *did* say. So, also, the writings of the fathers of the Golden Age of Lutheran Orthodoxy show us what was actually passed down to the generations immediately following the Reformation; if we would correct or elaborate upon them, it must not be by setting aside what they clearly teach and what was received by those generations as orthodox.

In the matter at hand, there is a substantive—and, indeed, substantial—difference between the understanding of Justification between the earlier Lutheran theologians and some later theologians of the Synodical Conference.

Thesis 7

While we may have had a 'received body of doctrine' beyond Scripture and the Confessions in a previous body of affiliation, the lack of ownership of the documents setting forth the same—and, thus, our inability to modify such non-binding documents where they have misspoken—prevents us from adopting the same as our own in such a way as to make them settlers of disputes. That is, the only way to adopt a non-binding document over which we do not have ownership (and, thus, cannot alter) is to adopt it as unalterable and binding; any other adoption is simultaneously both a burden and a waxen nose. Indeed, the Confessions are subscribed *in toto* and as is (that is, therefore, *quia*), since there is no other way truly to subscribe them.

Thesis 8

It is helpful to understand how a new (or refined) formulation of an article came to be—or, absent that insight, to see how one might have seen justification for the new terminology in that which already existed. "Objective Justification" may charitably be seen as a development from what Lutheran orthodoxy confessed concerning the Throne of Grace (*Gnadenthron;* i.e., the Mercy Seat, i.e., Christ), the 'new location' at which the sinner may be judged due to the Christ's bearing of all sin, rather than being judged at the seat of justice by the Law.[12]

Yet, "Objective Justification" is a gross overstatement of this concept. The creation of such an alternate place of judgment in Christ has the same effect for the sinner (in terms of providing an already-established reality to which one can look and which can be given through the Means of Grace) as would the postulating of a forensic declaration of mankind's righteousness, but without the unfortunate baggage[13] of the latter and in accord with the

12 Cf., e.g., Aegidius Hunnius: "Justification is the act of God by which He deigns to consider the man who is frightened by the awareness of sins and who flees to the Throne of Grace with pure mercy, through and for the sake of the merit of Christ, apprehended by faith; and, having forgiven him his sins, He reckons him as righteous, free from damnation, and also an heir of eternal life, without any human merit and without any view of God toward the virtues or the works of man" (as quoted in Rydecki, "The Forensic Appeal to the Throne of Grace," p. 20). So, Chemnitz: "The meaning of the word 'justify' in this article is judicial, namely, that the sinner, accused by the Law of God, convicted, and subjected to the sentence of eternal damnation, fleeing in faith to the throne of grace, is absolved for Christ's sake, reckoned and declared righteous, received into grace, and accepted to eternal life. And although John does not employ the word 'justify,' yet he describes the doctrine in judicial terms: 'He that believes is not judged; he does not come into judgment.' 'He sent His Son into the world, not that He should judge the world.' And 1 John 3: 'We have passed from death to life.' In Acts 3 Peter says that 'sins are blotted out.' Paul explains this when he says, Col. 2, that the hand writing which was against us has been blotted out." (*Examination,* Vol. 1, 474).

13 "Baggage"; that is, the baggage of asserting a justification apart from faith, which the fathers expressly rejected:

> Hence Paul, when he expressly discusses justification in Romans 3 and 4, does not know of a justification apart from faith, and especially as Galatians 2 plainly says, "Man is not justified except by faith in Jesus Christ." (Hunnius, *Theses Opposed to Huberianism*, Concerning Justification, Thesis 6)
>
> "*But how did the righteousness of Christ overflow to all men for justifica-*

clear 'mercy seat' language of both Testaments (Cf. Exodus 25:22; Hebrews 9:5 and Romans 3:25; 1 John 2:2, etc.).[14]

tion, since not all men are justified? We reply: The Apostle is not talking about the application of the benefit, but about the acquisition of the benefit. If we want to descend to the application, that universality must be restricted to those who are grafted into Christ by faith. For as the unrighteousness of Adam is communicated to all those who are descended from him by carnal generation, so the righteousness of Christ is communicated to all those who are grafted into Him through faith and spiritual regeneration." (Gerhard, *Adnotationes*, on Rom. 5:18)

"3) If we wanted to go beyond the limits of the Apostolic comparison, someone could infer from the same that the righteousness of Christ is propagated to us through carnal generation, since the unrighteousness of Adam is communicated to us in that manner. Likewise, one could infer that the righteousness of Christ is propagated to all men together, without any regard for faith or unbelief, since the sin of Adam is propagated to all through carnal generation.

"4) But since that is absurd, a distinction must fully be made between the acquisition and the application of the merit of Christ; or between the benefit itself and participation in the benefit. The acquisition of the merit, or the benefit itself obtained by the death of Christ is general. For as Adam, by his disobedience, enveloped all of his posterity in the guilt of sin, so Christ, who suffered and died for the sins of all, also merited and acquired righteousness for all. But this benefit is only applied to those who are grafted into Christ by faith, and only they become participants in this benefit." (*Adnotationes*, Rom. 5:19)

Note, then: when Hunnius and Gerhard say that St. Paul knew of no justification apart from faith and that the righteousness of Christ being propagated to all men (i.e., a general, universal, or objective justification) is "absurd," this is no mere treatment of the verses under consideration in a narrow use that allows for a broader use, but a declaration that a 'broader use' is not tenable.

14 We note that the Rev. Dr. Robert Preus also came to this conclusion late in his life, writing in his posthumously-published *Justification and Rome* (St. Louis, Concordia Academic Press, 1997):

Although Christ has acquired for us the remission of sins, justification, and sonship, God just the same does not justify us prior to our faith. Nor do we become God's children in Christ in such a way that justification in the mind of God takes place before we believe. (*Justification and Rome*, p. 132, quoted approvingly from Calov, *Apodixis Articulorum Fidei*, Lueneburg, 1684)

Quenstedt says, It is not the same thing to say, "Christ's righteousness

Thesis 9

It must always be remembered that something may be acceptable as a homiletical/rhetorical device that is inappropriate if passed off as exegesis—and completely improper if asserted as doctrine. As we are warned not to push a parable beyond its point/ground of comparison, even more we must remember that every illustration or analogy developed by Man will fall short and, while it may be helpful pedagogically, such language must not be made into a necessary part of our confession.

---

is imputed to us" and to say "Christ is our righteousness." For the imputation did not take place when Christ became our righteousness. The righteousness of Christ is the effect of His office. The imputation is the application of the effect of His office. The one, however, does not do away with the other. Christ is our righteousness effectively when He justifies us. His righteousness is ours objectively because our faith rests in Him. His righteousness is ours formally in that His righteousness is imputed to us. (*Justification and Rome,* p. 132, where fn. 76 gives the source as *Systema*, Par. III, Cap. 8, S. 2, q. 5, *Observatio* 19 (II, 787))

When does the imputation of Christ's righteousness take place? It did not take place when Christ, by doing and suffering, finished the work of atonement and reconciled the world to God. Then and there, when the sins of the world were imputed to Him and He took them, Christ became our righteousness and procured for us remission of sin, justification, and eternal life. "By thus making satisfaction He procured and merited (*acquisivit et promeruit*) for each and every man remission of all sins, exemption from all punishments of sin, grace and peace with God, eternal righteousness and salvation." (*Justification and Rome,* p. 131, where in fn. 74 Preus gives the source of the quote and this note: "*Systema*, Par. II, Cap.3, Memb. 2 S. 1, Th. 44 (II, 363). Cf. Abraham Calov, *Apodixis Articulorum Fidei* (Lueneburg, 1684), 249: 'Although Christ has acquired for us the remission of sins, justification, and sonship, God just the same does not justify us prior to our faith. Nor do we become God's children in Christ in such a way that justification in the mind of God takes place before we believe.'")

But the imputation of Christ's righteousness to the sinner takes place when the Holy Spirit brings him to faith through Baptism and the Word of the Gospel. Our sins were imputed to Christ at His suffering and death, imputed objectively after He, by His active and passive obedience, fulfilled and *procured* all righteousness for us. But the imputation of His righteousness to us takes place when we are brought to faith. (*Justification and Rome,* p. 72)

Thesis 10

In a similar fashion, we must make a distinction between an exegetical conclusion (no matter how sound) and a direct statement by the Lord in His Word. This need for a distinction is not to lessen the authority of an article that is arrived at by reasoning from the Scriptures (e.g., the article of the Holy and Blessed God as Triune), but to keep from misstating *how* the article is taught in God's Word and, possibly, becoming guilty of putting words into the Lord's mouth that He has not Himself given us and coming under His proper condemnation for so doing ("I am against the prophets," says the Lord, "who use their own tongues but say, 'He says,'" Jeremiah 23:31).[15]

Thesis 11

For example, to say,[16] "Christ was absolved in the resurrection," is to employ an illustration that is not truly apt, as an 'absolution' declares one innocent in spite of one's guilt and inability to pay for his transgressions, but the Christ's 'justification' is, rather, the vindication of One who both is innocent by nature and by conduct and who has paid for the sins of all others. The fact that the Christ was made sin for us (2 Corinthians 5:21) and bore our sins as His own (Psalm 69:5) does not require Him to be absolved, since, again, He was not forgiven for our sins (forgiveness requiring someone else to pay the debt). Instead, He Himself paid the debt.

15 "Scripture teaches" has a different impact, breeds a different expectation, and requires a different method of establishment from "God says." Scripture *teaches* that God is Triune, but it never *says* that He is.

16 As those who might be cited by both parties have done, e.g., both Gerhard and Walther, even though Gerhard (cf. the second footnote to Thesis 8, above) calls what has come to be known as "Objective Justification" an "absurd" idea.

Thesis 12

Rather, by the Christ's vindication, absolution is won and, indeed, created for us. That is, by His bearing the judgment for our sin upon the cross, He has made a new way—a new 'place'—for our judgment to take place: rather than the judgment of Sinai,[17] we are judged at the Throne of Grace, where the Christ's perfect active obedience is credited to us because His perfect passive obedience has made payment for all sin. Christ is Himself our absolution and apart from Him there can be no absolution.

Thesis 13

Thus, to make the 'justification of the Christ' in any way similar to our justification in connection with Christ is to cheapen the merit of Christ.[18]

Thesis 14

Again, to make the justification of the sinner anything less than the 'justification of the Christ' is to cheapen the merit of Christ.[19]

Thesis 15

We must distinguish between what a passage could, conceivably, mean, what it most probably means, and what it must mean. Failure to do so leads to eisegesis and the amassing of passages that 'could possibly fit' under either understanding being used as if they proved

---

17 The judgment of our thoughts, words, and deeds not squaring with God's description of the attributes of His People in the Tables He handed down on Sinai.

18 Since His justification is won by His own righteousness, whereas ours is given to us apart from any righteousness of our own.

19 Since what the justified have is the very righteousness of Christ Himself.

one's point and, worse, using those that definitely do not fit as if they were intending to say something that they do not. Such is the case with, e.g., the ELS's explanation of the Small Catechism, where Question 210 asks, "Why do we say, 'I believe in the forgiveness of sins?'" and answers, "...because the Bible assures us that God the Father has by grace forgiven all sinners and declared them righteous in Christ," and attempts to use Romans 3:24 (as presented, "*[All]* are justified freely by His grace...") in a way that completely divorces it from its context.[20]

Thesis 16

Again, the language of "Objective Justification"—not just the term itself, now, but the statement of the formula in its various aspects, is troubling in several ways, as shall be discussed in the next several theses, along with the terminology. The language with which we present an article of doctrine must accurately and carefully exhibit what is in God's Word; the language must not (inasmuch as it lies within us in our speaking) mislead the hearer into thinking that he will find a direct statement in Scripture when one does not exist or that he will find an expression there that it does not, in fact, contain.

Thesis 17

As much as possible, Biblical terms should be used only to express what they mean in the Bible (cf. the term 'elder'). Further, we should use Biblical terms and illustrations to express and proclaim scriptural truth. (While "of one substance with the Father" was, finally, necessary

---

20 *Catechism & Explanation: An Explanation of Dr. Martin Luther's Small Catechism,* 2001, Evangelical Lutheran Synod, Mankato, MN. Question #210 is found on p. 143.

and has been our common terminology for over 1,500 years, the reticence initially to use a non-biblical term was good and right. God gave His Word to tell us about Himself; as much as possible, we should use what He has given us there.) Even if a Biblical term has a long history of being misused (e.g., 'deacon'), that misuse must not be allowed to continue in our own teaching, as so doing perpetuates the associated errors.

Thesis 18

Thus, asserting the existence of a forensic declaration by God that is not stated in Scripture is to say what God does not say and to attribute it to Him; if there is no direct statement,[21] it is an attempt to delve into God's secret counsel (*Deus absconditus*). To proclaim an action as a forensic declaration, there must be actual evidence of such a declaration—preferably a direct quote—and not simply a matter of conjecture, no matter how well-founded we believe that conjecture to be. Especially is this so when such a concept is first put forth by those who live nearly two millennia after the event and when those who are ostensibly their fathers in the faith have never made such a declaration concerning the whole world of sinners. (Cf. the second footnote to Thesis 21.)

Thesis 19

So, also, language such as "there took place a change in the heart of God," which, unlike language as-

21 The fathers we have cited and will cite were wise enough to see this and to pull back from overreaching, as we see with Luther's correction on p, 286 of his 1535 lectures on Galatians (*AE*, vol. 26) to what he said on p. 280 that is wrongly used by some to accuse him of teaching what he did not teach regarding Justification. As St. Paul warns, "learn in us not to think beyond what is written." (1 Corinthians 4:6, NKJV)

serting a new 'place' of judgment,[22] is an anthropomorphism that denies God's immutability and/or the full participation of all the Persons of the Blessed and Holy Trinity in the willing and working of salvation (*opera ad extra trinitatis indivisa sunt*). If it was foreordained in the counsel of the Holy Trinity that God the Son should be sent forth to do the work that He did, there is no 'change in God's heart,' but a change of the 'place' of judgment that is a fulfillment of what He has willed from before the foundation of the world,[23] an avenue through which a righteousness apart from the Law now avails,[24] by means of which God sees the sinner and the sinner sees God differently from the view that comes through Mt. Sinai.

Thesis 20

As asserted earlier, Thesis 19 says and gives everything that "Objective Justification" would attempt to say and give, but without changing God or putting words into His mouth. It holds forth not a pre-existing forensic declaration (which is not recorded in Scripture) about the world being without sin, but simply the merit of Christ (and the assurance of the sinner's righteousness thereby) that is the proper object of faith, as is clear from the early Lutheran exegetes and dogmaticians.[25]

---

22 The Throne of Grace, which is nothing other than Christ and His merit, which is the fulfillment of the Old Testament Mercy Seat, by which name Christ is both called and referred to in the New Testament. (Cf. Exodus 25:22; Hebrews 9:5 and Romans 3:25; 1 John 2:2, etc.)

23 Cf. Revelation 13:8, which makes it clear that our salvation was already "in God's heart" before He created the world.

24 Romans 3:21,22; note that v. 22 defines the term from v. 21 and may not be artificially separated from it.

25 We commend to the reader the Rev. Paul Rydecki's "The Forensic Appeal to the Throne of Grace," especially to the quotes which appear in each appendix to that essay (as well as in its body). Unlike the snippets gener-

Thesis 21

Regarding the proper object of faith: ought it be a *pre-existing declaration/judicial pronouncement* of forgiveness (without words) or the *acquisition* of a judicial pronouncement of forgiveness? The latter has much testimony among our theologians prior to 1850, while the former is asserted with such vehemence by, e.g., Pieper,[26] that it is said that the Gospel is gone altogether if such an assertion is not made. Such an assertion about this formulation that seems unknown (other than as something to be condemned as a part of Huber's error) prior to the mid-19th century,[27] is not only ridiculous on its face, but injurious to the Church, as it disparages the orthodox Lutheran fathers and leads to parochialism and disrespect for older Lutheran writings that is so prevalent today.[28]

Thesis 22

Regarding the proper object of faith: ought it be a *pre-existing declaration/judicial pronouncement* of forgive-

---

ally adduced by those who wish eisegetically to find the Lutheran fathers as supporters of "Objective Justification," Pastor Rydecki translates the *context* around such quotes, as well, and thereby demonstrates that those who would thus push the fathers into their service do so unfairly. The paper is available at http://tinyurl.com/n28ndt6

26 *Christian Dogmatics,* II:349–351

27 See the second footnote to Thesis 24.

28 If an appeal were made to Luther's comments in his lectures on Galatians (AE, Vol. 26, p. 280), that in Christ's death the world was set free from sin without reference to faith, one must also concede that there is no longer any death, as "death is conquered and abolished in the whole world so that now it is nothing but a picture of death," except that Luther makes his intent clear when he says (p. 285), "I believe in the holy church." This is plainly nothing else than if we were to say, 'I believe that there is no sin and no death in the church.'" So, also, (p. 286) "Therefore, wherever there is faith in Christ, there sin has in fact been abolished, put to death, and buried. But where there is no faith in Christ, there sin remains."

ness (without any recording of God making such a pronouncement) or change in the heart of the immutable God without His saying that His heart has changed, or the *acquisition* of a judicial pronouncement of forgiveness and a new venue (Christ, the Mercy Seat) through which such a declaration may be received? In either case, there is an *already made* 'thing' to be communicated and trusted in; the difference is that the first two do not have specific testimony from Scripture to such an effect, while the later does.[29]

Thesis 23

Concerning the above, those trying to assert "Objective Justification" are often inconsistent, speaking of the acquisition of a pronouncement of righteousness at times and apparently not realizing that it is *not* the same as such a pronouncement itself.[30] Yet, this is the beauty of the thing and a further demonstration that the acquisition of God's declaration is not only the correct position, but that it provides that for which it is often asserted that "Objective Justification" is necessary.[31]

---

29 Cf. Hebrews 9:5 and Romans 3:25; 1 John 2:2, etc.

30 "Pronouncement of righteousness" = "justification." "Objective Justification" does not say that such a pronouncement has 'merely' been acquired, but that it has already been levied.

31 Note that "the acquisition of a pronouncement of righteousness" without the assertion that such a declaration has already been made does *not* reduce said acquisition to that of a "potential pronouncement" in any way other than one might say that the prophecies that a Serpent-crushing Seed of the Woman or One Born of a Virgin spoke (merely) to a 'potential fulfillment'. *The prophecies and promises of God are just as certain when they are made as when they are fulfilled.* Rather, the acquisition itself gives the 'substance' that is given through the Means of Grace, creating faith so that justification is truly received.

Thesis 24

We ought not think that Walther[32] (and Schaller[33] and Hoenecke[34]), Pieper, *et alii,* who formulated the current expressions of "Objective Justification" were unfamiliar with either Huber[35] or Aegidius Hunnius.[36,37] The question is how dependent upon Huber they were, since they specifically distanced themselves from him. That is, did they see themselves as accidentally using the same terminology or did they intentionally adopt it while seeking to remove the parts of his teaching that they knew were offensive and keep the rest?[38] That such terminol-

32 Cf. the first footnote of Thesis 2, above.

33 "The doctrine of universal, socalled objective justification sets forth that the Lord God by grace because of Christ's redemption actually forgave sins to all men." Cf., "Salvation is just as perfect and complete for those who are finally lost. This is the only reason, but a sufficient one, why he that believeth not is damned. Unbelief is the rejection of life and salvation achieved and personally intended for every unbeliever." (Schaller, John. *Biblical Christology*. Milwaukee: Northwestern Publishing House, 1982. Cited by Beckman, who begins the paragraph in which the first quote occurs, with the comment, "The term 'objective justification' is little more than 100 years old in our Lutheran circles." "Universal and Objective Justification with Special Emphasis on a Recent Controversy," David J. Beckman, delivered at the District Pastor-Teacher Conference of the South Atlantic District (WELS), January 27, 1983, p. 3. "Socalled"—rather than "so-called"—is from Beckman's text.)

34 "The objective act of justification and the subjective possession and enjoyment thereof in blessed peace." (*Dogmatik,* Cited by Beckman, ibid.)

35 See the footnote to Thesis 3.

36 Aegidius Hunnius (1550–1603) was brought to Wittenberg as a professor in 1592. He was also superintendent and oversaw the visitation of the churches of Saxony, coauthoring the Saxon Visitation Articles.

37 In fact, Pieper quotes Hunnius seven times in volume two of *Christian Dogmatics*—always positively—but never cites him concerning this topic, and brushes him aside in volume three with regard to the Lutheran understanding of election.

38 Compare this with what modern 'Lutherans' do with the hymns of false teachers, church growth methodology, and the like. One might ask a similar question with regard to Walther's aberrations regarding the Office

ogy would be adopted with a specific rejection of what were seen as Huber's excesses, instead of simply rejecting the terminology merits further investigation. In any case, while they seek to distance themselves from Huber's error, their insistence on a dogmatic assertion that is so foreign to those who came before as to necessitate such distancing is evidence of its novelty.

Thesis 25

Defenses of "Objective Justification"[39] quite often contain a statement of how unfortunate it is that this term has come into use—which one would not expect with a truly useful and unencumbered term. Both because of the earlier use by Huber and because of the number of true and false definitions with which the term has been associated, it ought to be discarded, as its use brings no clarity.[40]

---

of the Ministry and church polity, namely whether, e.g., Walther was simply overreacting against Stephan and, later, Grabau, or was trying to purify Vehse so that he would not have to live with practices that were openly confessing a false understanding of the Church and the Office. *In any case, Walther's understanding of Church and Ministry contained error and that error grew in the century that followed him precisely because his work was the foundation and touchstone for those promoting subsequent error.* In a similar fashion, the overstatement that is (Waltherian) "Objective Justification" leads to errors that Walther himself would have in no way endorsed, but that should have been expected.

39 At least by Lutheran Church—Missouri Synod writers; Wisconsin Evangelical Lutheran Synod writers do not seem to have any qualms about the terminology.

40 Thus: Kurt Marquart in his paper concerning Larry Darby, p. 1 (available through various web sites, including http://angelfire.com/ny4/lutherantheology.marquartjustification.html), where he quotes Henry Hamaan's similar sentiment in *Justification by Faith in Modern Theology*, Graduate Study 2 (St. Louis: School for Graduate Studies, Concordia Seminary, 1957), p. 60; Jon Buchholz in his essay at the 2005 WELS synodical convention, p. 3, fn. 4; the LCMS's response to the Joint Declaration on the Doctrine of Justification, *The Joint Declaration on the Doctrine of Justification in Confessional Lutheran Perspective*, p. 24–25, similarly; all of these speak of a preference for

Thesis 26

Moreover, as we are admonished in the first Article of the Formula of Concord, "As regards terms and expressions, it is best and safest to use and retain the form of sound words employed concerning this [or any] article in the Holy Scriptures and the above-mentioned books," (Thorough Declaration I:50) we ought not invent new terminology or restate any article of doctrine without specific need or in any way that contradicts that "form of sound words," much less do so in a way that eisegetically deals with older writings to force them to 'support' the new formulation, or that requires regurgitation of a formula that is not proven to be in accord with what the Confessions were understood to teach by the theologians of Lutheran orthodoxy.

Nonetheless, the discussion is not about the term, but about the teaching—but the term is to be discarded as (at best) a parochial neologism of the (long-defunct) Evangelical Lutheran Synodical Conference of North America, claimed as much by those in the bodies that made up said conference who do not really teach "Objective Justification" as by those who do.

Thesis 27

The sins of all men have been imputed to Christ and He was punished (completely) for them all, so that He rightly said, "It is finished"—the taking of the punishment was complete and the store of both active and passive obedience was fulfilled. Nonetheless, Holy Scripture does not teach that mankind is now seen as sinless apart from or prior to faith, but only that God's desire is to judge them through the Mercy Seat or Throne of Grace,

---

other terms to be used, and there are others that could be cited.

which is Christ: those not so judged are still dead in their sins, as St. Paul says of the Ephesians (2:1), etc., as Luther also clearly teaches. (cf. Vol. 26, p. 285–286)[41]

Thesis 28

The reconciliation/justification of the world is already accomplished in Christ in this sense: that what God needs in order to consider each sinner righteous—the exchange of righteousness for sin in Christ—is accomplished; yet, unless the sinner is reconciled to God/justified by God through trust in the righteousness of Christ (cf. 2 Cor. 5), he is not indeed reconciled. Since some are not reconciled/justified, it cannot be said that all are reconciled/justified.[42]

Thesis 29

The orthodox Lutheran position, as easily demonstrated from the fathers of the Age of Lutheran Orthodoxy, is that by the resurrection Christ is declared the Son of God with power and is vindicated (shown to be righteous by merit), by having borne the sins of all mankind and suffered for them until there was nothing left to punish, His righteousness now avails for every sinner and He—with His merit and the promise attached thereto—is the proper object of our faith. It is through faith in this promise alone that the sinner stands justified before God,

---

41 As previously shown, Luther by no means teaches a universal justification in these pages, nor those that go before, as he specifically says "where there is no faith in Christ, there sin remains." (*AE*, Vol. 26, p. 286)

42 It would be wrong to claim that the first half of the first sentence in this Thesis presents "Objective Justification"; by such an assertion, the true definition of said doctrine would be violated, as "Objective Justification" does not merely state "that what God needs in order to consider each sinner righteous—the exchange of righteousness for sin in Christ—is accomplished," but that the whole world has, indeed, already been declared righteous and that no sin remains.

since he is now judged at the Mercy Seat, the Throne of Grace, so that God sees him as entirely righteous in connection with Christ.

Conclusion

If all that were meant by "Objective Justification" were the acquisition of righteousness for all mankind so that there is a basis for God to declare an individual righteous through the God-given gift of faith receiving God's pledge to consider him entirely righteous and forgiven purely for the sake of Christ, we would merely caution against the term.[43] Since, however, it is more than that—the declaration that all mankind is sinless before God before and apart from faith in Christ—this teaching is not only dangerous in its grossest abuse (crass universalism), but is in itself contrary to God's Word and the exhibition of the same by the Symbols of Christ's Church.

That the foregoing theses correctly reflect the doctrine of the symbolical books is demonstrated by the writings of the earliest generations of orthodox teachers of the faith confessed in the Book of Concord. Thus, the doctrine of "Objective Justification" (both the teaching and its terminology) is hereby rejected.

43 "Objective Justification" is, at best, an ambiguous term by virtue of the various ways it is represented by those claiming to adhere to it; thus, it is terminology that has no place in the Church. As with the Sacraments, in which we maintain the words and elements given us by Christ so that no element of doubt is introduced, language cannot be ambiguous lest the Church is given place to fall into "false belief, despair, and other great shame and vice." Both such ambiguity in the use of the term "Objective Justification" and the false teaching advanced in the historical usage of this term (whether that of Huber or that of the theologians of the former Synodical Conference), has led even those among us who formerly made use of it to abandon the continued use of this term in the Church in connection with our desire to reject the false teaching associated with it.

These theses, like those which our diocese has previously written and agreed to, are not seen by us as additions to our vows to the Scriptures and the Lutheran Confessions, which vows are unconditional. These theses may change as the issues are further clarified. However, we do see them as defining the limits of our fellowship with regard to these issues until such time as we are convinced otherwise from the Scriptures and Lutheran Confessions, or until further clarification is needed. We are keenly aware of the fluid nature of such statements. We are also keenly aware of the clear lines of distinction they draw among those who call themselves Lutherans, and we intend to draw such lines.

These theses are not a declaration of fellowship. Those inside our fellowship voluntarily agree with these theses and support them, but we also wish to have these theses function as a marker of agreement between Christians who are not yet necessarily in fellowship. Therefore, we invite all who agree with these theses to express their agreement without necessarily committing themselves to fellowship.

We hope and pray that these theses will be yet another building block in establishing a more healthy and orthodox Lutheran Church in our time, and in this country. With this hope, we, with joy and profound thanks to our triune God, accept and confess these theses.

Version 3.2 — Text as Unanimously Approved by the Diocese
The Beheading of John the Baptist, 29 August 2013

The Forensic Appeal to the Throne of Grace

in the Theology of the Lutheran Age of Orthodoxy:

A Reflection on Atonement and Its Relationship to Justification

by Rev. Paul A. Rydecki

presented at the colloquium of the
Evangelical Lutheran Diocese of North America
Malone, Texas
April 30, 2013

The Christian article of the sinner's justification before God is explained in countless tomes of theological writings, and with good reason. This chief article of the Christian faith is the thick trunk of the tree that is the Christian faith. Like the deeds of Christ Himself, the points of doctrine that sprout from this tree and the applications of it are so numerous that, "if they were written one by one, I suppose that even the world itself could not contain the books that would be written" (Jn. 21:25).

And yet, the article of justification itself has been condensed down to a single (divinely inspired) Volume for us. It is further encapsulated, both eloquently and abundantly, in the first of the Pauline Epistles to grace our Bibles. And it can be summarized so briefly and so simply that a child can grasp it.

"For God so loved the world that He gave His only begotten Son, that whoever believes in Him should not perish but have everlasting life. For God did not send His Son into the world to condemn the world, but that the world through Him might be saved. He who believes in Him is not condemned; but he who does not believe is condemned already, because he has not believed in the name of the only begotten Son of God" (Jn. 3:16-18 - NKJV).

The Lutherans from the age of orthodoxy[1] understood the simplicity of the article of justification. While that understanding did not curtail their verbosity, all of their writings on the chief article were nothing more than elaborations on a common theme, the fleshing out of a few points of a common outline that remained unchanged from the time of Luther through the time of Gerhard.

The problem in the Lutheran Church in our age is not that too little has been said since the age of Lutheran orthodoxy, but too much. The outline has, in some cases, been sup-

1 For our purposes, the age of Lutheran orthodoxy will be defined as the period beginning with Martin Luther and ending with Johann Gerhard, c. AD 1515-1637.

planted; the concept, blurred. I hope to demonstrate in this essay the level of clarity, consistency and precision that once characterized the Lutheran presentation of the doctrine of justification. My contribution here will be minimal, as I intend to let the Blessed Fathers speak for themselves through their writings, in which we will explore their concept of the Biblical teaching of justification, noting especially the distinctions they make between the atonement that Christ has accomplished for all sinners and the justification of the sinner that only takes place as a result of a forensic appeal to the Throne of Grace.

The Common Outline of Forensic Justification

A "common outline" was mentioned above. One may speak of points of an outline, constituent elements, essential components, or simply the "causes" that are necessary and belonging to the article of justification. In any case, it is presented succinctly in FC:SD:III:24-25:

> If the article of justification is to remain pure, the greatest attention must be given with special diligence. Otherwise, what comes before faith, and what follows after it, will be mixed together or inserted into the article of justification as necessary and belonging to it. For it is not one and the same thing to talk about conversion and to talk about justification.
>
> Not everything that belongs to conversion also belongs to the article of justification. Only God's grace, Christ's merit, and faith belong and are necessary to the article of justification. Faith receives these blessings in the promise of the Gospel, by which Christ's righteousness is credited to us. From this we receive and have forgiveness of sins, reconciliation with God, sonship, and are made heirs of eternal life.

From these words, one can identify four necessary components in the basic outline of a sinner's justification: 1) God's grace, 2) Christ's merit, 3) faith, through which the righteousness of Christ is imputed to the sinner, and 4) the promise of the Gospel, since faith is only kindled in the heart by the Holy Spirit working through the Word.

The role of each of these components is described by all of the principal writers in the age of orthodoxy in "forensic," that is, "judicial" or "courtroom" terminology, as they unfold the Biblical concept of "justification."

Luther combines the analogy of the sinner standing before God's judgment seat with the sinner taking shelter under Christ, as a chick takes shelter under a mother-hen:

> I mentioned above in an Epistle that it was not enough for us to be pious, do good works, and live in grace; not even our righteousness, much less our unrighteousness, may stand up before the eyes of God and his judgment. Therefore I have said: faith, if it is true faith, is such that it does not rely on itself, on its believing, but it holds on to Christ and shelters itself under his righteousness; it lets this righteousness be its shelter and shield, even as the chick does not rely on its life and speed, but seeks shelter under the mother-hen's body and wings. To survive before God's judgment seat, it is not enough for one to say: I believe and have received grace; for everything within him is unable to protect him sufficiently. Rather he holds up to this judgment Christ's own righteousness; he lets it deal with God's judgment and it stands up for him forever with all honors, as Psalms 111[:3] and 112[:3, 9] say: "His righteousness endures forever." Under this righteousness he creeps, snuggles, and crouches; he trusts and believes and does not doubt that it will keep him protected. Then it also comes to pass that way, and he is preserved through this same faith, not for the sake of faith, but for the sake of Christ and his righteousness, under whose protection he is living. It also follows that faith which does not act in this manner is not the true faith. (*Luther's Works, Vol. 52*, 96)

Melanchthon, writing in the Apology:

> Furthermore, in this passage, to justify means (accord-

ing to court language) to acquit a guilty person and declare him righteous. But this happens because of the righteousness of another, namely, of Christ. This righteousness is communicated to us through faith. Therefore, since our righteousness in this passage is the credit of the righteousness of another, we must here speak about righteousness in a way different than in philosophy or in a civil court. (There we seek after the righteousness of one's own work, which certainly is in the will.) So Paul says in 1 Corinthians 1:30, "He is the source of your life in Christ Jesus, whom God made our wisdom and our righteousness and sanctification and redemption." And in 2 Corinthians 5:21, "For our sake He made Him to be sin who knew no sin, so that in Him we might become the righteousness of God." But because Christ's righteousness is given to us through faith, faith is righteousness credited to us. In other words, it is that by which we are made acceptable to God on account of the credit and ordinance of God, as Paul says, "Faith is counted as righteousness" (Romans 4:3, 5). (Ap:V:184-186)

The Formula of Concord:

A person cannot stand with and ‹on the ground of this righteousness› [that is, the righteousness of new obedience] before God's court. Before God's court only the righteousness of Christ's obedience, suffering, and death—which is credited to faith—can stand. So only for the sake of this obedience is the person pleasing and acceptable to God and received into adoption and made an heir of eternal life. (FC:SD:III:32)

Chemnitz:

The meaning of the word "justify" in this article is judicial, namely, that the sinner, accused by the Law of God, convicted, and subjected to the sentence of eternal damnation, fleeing in faith to the throne of grace, is absolved for Christ's sake, reckoned and declared righteous, received into grace, and accepted to eternal life. And although John does not employ the word "justify," yet he describes the doctrine in judicial terms: "He that believes is not judged; he does not come into judgment."

"He sent His Son into the world, not that He should judge the world." And 1 John 3: "We have passed from death to life." In Acts 3 Peter says that "sins are blotted out." Paul explains this when he says, Col. 2, that the hand writing which was against us has been blotted out. (*Examination*, Vol. 1, 474).

Gerhard:

The verb δικαιοῦσθαι has a forensic meaning, to be pronounced righteous, to be absolved, since the whole act of our justification is described with forensic terms. The *defendant* is man the sinner; the *plaintiff*, or the accuser, is the law and the devil; the *witness* is the conscience; the *advocate* is Christ; the *judge* is God. Both accusation and condemnation are contrasted with this justification. (*Adnotationes ad priora capita Epistolae D. Pauli ad Romanos*, Romans 3:24, translation mine.)

(5) The contrast is evident in this apostolic text between justification and condemnation, v. 16 and v.18. But since they are contrasted under the same genre, and condemnation is, to be sure, a judicial act, from which it follows that justification is also a judicial act, and hence it consists, not in the infusion of righteousness, but in the absolution from sins. Undoubtedly, as through the sin of Adam sin is propagated to all men, for it results in condemnation for them, that is, because of it they are damned by the righteous judgment of God unless reconciliation and remission take place, so through the merit of Christ righteousness and salvation have been obtained for all, so that they may be justified by faith, that is, that they may be pronounced righteous, absolved from sins and freed from condemnation.

(6) To be made righteous and to be justified are considered by the Apostle to be equivalent expressions. Therefore, to be made righteous is contrasted with "for condemnation" in v.19; so also "to be justified" in v.18; and hence each has a forensic meaning. The verb "they will be made" indicates that these things are carried out before the tribunal of God's righteous judgment, who condemns Adam's posterity on account of sin, but absolves believers in Christ from that dam-

nation and makes them righteous (Rom. 10:3, 2 Cor. 5:21). (*Adnotationes*, Rom. 5:19, translation mine.)

Aegidius Hunnius, in his *Articulus de iustificatione hominis peccatoris gratuita*:

> *What does the word "justify" mean in the present discussion?*
>
> In a human judgment, they are said "to be justified" who are pronounced free from the guilt of the crimes of which they were accused. (The Scripture speaks in this sense in Deut. 25: If a case arises and they go to judgment, the righteous man should be justified and the ungodly man condemned, as this word "justifying" is understood in both Proverbs 17 and Is. 5). In the same way, understanding the word in the same forensic usage, they are said to be justified before God who, fleeing to the Throne of Grace[2], are absolved from the guilt of sin and from damnation, and are reckoned as righteous by the imputation of the righteousness of Christ, which consists in His obedience (p.17, translation mine).

A Common Analogy to Explain the Common Outline

The last citation above from Aegidius Hunnius briefly expresses an analogy that was commonly used among the Lutheran Fathers to describe forensic justification. Gerhard used it[3]. Luther used it as well[4]. It is essentially an expansion of

---

2 Latin: *thronum gratiae*. Luther had translated the Greek word ἱλαστήριον ("propitiation, propitiatorium, Mercy Seat," or "sacrifice of atonement" in the NIV) in Rom. 3:25 with "Gnadenstuhl." Elsewhere it is rendered "Gnadenthron."

3 In his commentary on Romans 3:22-26, explaining how Christ is the "Propitiatorium," the antitype of the Old Testament Mercy Seat.

4 Luther: "[We know] about the unfathomable goodness and mercy of our heavenly Father: that Jesus Christ is our mediator, our throne of grace, and our bishop before God in heaven, who daily intercedes for us and reconciles all who believe in him alone, and who call upon him; that he is not a judge, nor cruel, except for those who do not believe in him, or who reject his comfort and grace; [and] that he is not the man who accuses and threatens us, but rather the man who reconciles us [with God], and intercedes for us

Romans 3:22-26. Chemnitz offers this analogy in its most extended form, depicting the various aspects of this courtroom setting. He alludes to it in his *Examination*, but fleshes out the presentation more thoroughly in his *Loci Theologici* and his *Enchiridion*. It is presented here at length, because it expresses so clearly the Lutheran concept of justification in relation to the atonement.

> Thus, the use of the legal term "justification" refutes the ideas of the Epicureans. For it shows that the justification of the sinner is not some insignificant or perfunctory thing, but that the whole human being stands before the judgment of God and is examined both with respect to his nature as well as his works, and this according to the norm of the divine law. But because after the entrance of sin a human being in this life does not have true and perfect conformity with the law of God, nothing is found in this examination, whether in the person's nature or in his works, that he can use to justify himself before God; rather the Law pronounces the sentence of condemnation, written by the very finger of God Himself.
>
> Now God does not justify the ungodly by some kind of mistake, as a judge often makes a faulty decision by failure to examine the evidence sufficiently or by wrong thinking; nor through indifference, as if He did not care about the transgression of His law; nor through wickedness, as if He approved of our iniquity, connived with it, or were in collusion with the impious. A justification of this kind God Himself pronounces to be an abomination, Ex. 23:1; Is. 5:23; Prov. 17:15. God cannot retract the sentence of condemnation revealed in the Law, unless it is perfectly satisfied or fulfilled, Matt. 5:18.
>
> Thus righteousness and satisfaction are required where God is to justify. Luther is correct when he says that God remits no sin unless the Law has been satisfied with re-

---

with his own death and blood shed for us so that we should not fear him, but approach him with all assurance and call him dear Savior, sweet Comforter, faithful bishop of our souls, etc." (Luther's Works, Vol. 50, 20-21).

gard to it. In the case of human judgment, to be sure, guilt is absolved either because of some preceding merit (for they are accounted worthy who deserve to be forgiven), or with respect to present righteousness and innocence either of the cause or of the person, or with respect to a satisfaction which the guilty party promises to make either to the judge or to his opponent in the case. But before God's judgment man can put up nothing in his own defense in order that he might be justified, as many very clear Scripture passages declare.

Therefore, because God does not justify out of frivolity, unconcern, error, or iniquity, nor because He finds anything in man whereby he might be justified before God; and yet the just requirement of the Law must be fulfilled in those who are to be justified[5], Rom. 8:4, therefore a foreign righteousness must intervene—the kind of righteousness which not only with payment of penalties but also with perfect obedience to the divine law made satisfaction in such a way that it could be a propitiation for the sins of the whole world.

To this the terrified sinner, condemned by the voice of the Law, flees in true faith. This he desires, begs for, lays hold of; to this he submits himself; this he uses as his defense before the judgment seat of God and against the accusation of the Law. By regard for this and by its imputation he is justified, that is, he is absolved from the comprehensive sentence of condemnation and receives the promise of eternal life. This is what Paul is saying in Rom. 3:31 : "The doctrine of the righteousness of faith does not destroy the Law but upholds it."

Paul clearly describes the act of justification in this way in Romans 3:

1. The conscience of the sinner is through the Law placed before the judgment tribunal of God (who is a consuming fire and in whose sight not even the stars are pure), is accused, convicted, and condemned, so that it is afflicted and pressed down by a terrifying sense of the wrath of God,

---

5 Latin: *in justificandis*

Rom. 3:19: "... that every mouth may be stopped and all the world may become guilty before God" [KJV].

2. The heart thus contrite does not entertain Epicurean thoughts but anxiously seeks whether and how it can be freed from the comprehensive sentence of condemnation. From such thoughts come such passages as Ps. 130:3: "If You should mark iniquities ...."; Ps. 143:2: "Enter not into judgment ..."; Rom. 7:24: "Who shall deliver me ...?" ...

3. Therefore God, "who is rich in mercy" [Eph. 2:4], has had mercy upon us and has set forth a propitiation through faith in the blood of Christ, and those who flee as suppliants to this throne of grace He absolves from the comprehensive sentence of condemnation, and by the imputation of the righteousness of His Son, which they grasp in faith, He pronounces them righteous, receives them into grace, and adjudges them to be heirs of eternal life.

This is certainly the judicial meaning of the word "justification," in almost the same way that a guilty man who has been sentenced before the bar of justice is acquitted.

It is manifest how much clarity this gives to the discussion of justification. The fathers in disputing this matter often spoke inadequately about justification. But in their devotional writings, when they were looking at the picture of the divine judgment or the divine judicial process, they handled the doctrine of this article very well.

The example of Bernard [of Clairvaux, 1091–1153] shows this clearly, because he was not involved in idle speculations but was exercising himself in the serious matter of repentance based on the doctrine and testimony of Paul. Gerson has some wonderful thoughts about the tribunal of God's justice and the throne of His grace. For if we are discussing our common position before the tribunal of God, we are all subject to the tribunal of His justice; and because before Him no living person can be justified but all are condemned, therefore God has also set up another tribunal, the throne of grace. And the Son of God pleads for us

> the benefit of being called away from the tribunal of justice to the throne of grace. Therefore the Pharisee, because he was not willing to use the benefit of this calling, but wanted to enter into judgment before the tribunal of justice, was condemned. But the publican, who was first accused at the tribunal of justice, convicted and condemned there, later by faith called out to the throne of grace and was justified [Luke 18:9–14]. (*Loci Theologici*, p.481-482)
>
> And this is the process or act of the justification of a sinner before the judgment seat of God, so that he appeals from the throne of the strict justice of God to the throne of grace in the blood of the Son of God, as Gerson describes the matter of justification by the apt simile of forensic appeal. (*Enchiridion*, Q. 146)
>
> All these points so beautifully illustrating the doctrine of justification come from the correct linguistic understanding of the word "justification." (*Loci Theologici*, p.482)

Several things must be noted here. First, that, on account of the satisfaction Christ made to the divine law, there exists, objectively, a Throne of Grace to which all sinners are invited (in the Gospel) to flee, an alternate place of judgment opened up as a result of God's grace and the obedience, suffering, death, and resurrection of Christ. It is "another tribunal," apart from the Law, where God is propitious, where absolution is pronounced, justification is declared, and eternal life is bestowed for the sake of Christ. The "atonement" made by Christ has opened up this Throne of Grace, which is actually Christ Himself, the "atonement cover" or "Mercy Seat," sprinkled with His own blood[6], the "Atoner" or "Reconciler."

Second, that justification occurs in the divine courtroom, not *without* the accused fleeing in faith to the Throne of Grace, not *before* the accused flees in faith to the Throne of

6 Gerhard, *Adnotationes* on Rom. 3:25: "The type of the sprinkling of the Propitiatorium with the blood of the sacrifices, by which was signified that our Propitiatorium in the New Testament was likewise to be sprinkled, not with the blood of another, but with His own blood."

Grace, but *simultaneously* with this "fleeing" or this "forensic appeal." This present-tense (that is, concurrent with faith) absolution and justification is perfectly in keeping with the language of the Augsburg Confession:

> Also they teach that men cannot be justified before God by their own strength, merits, or works, but are freely justified for Christ's sake, through faith, when they believe that they are received into favor, and that their sins are forgiven for Christ's sake, who, by His death, has made satisfaction for our sins. This faith God imputes for righteousness in His sight. Rom. 3 and 4.[7] (AC:IV)

> ...in them that hear the Gospel, to wit, that God, not for our own merits, but for Christ's sake, justifies those who believe that they are received into grace for Christ's sake (AC:V)

> Scripture teaches that we are justified before God, through faith in Christ, when we believe that our sins are forgiven for Christ's sake (AC:XXIV:28).

Third, that, although the foreign righteousness of Christ has made satisfaction to the divine law so that it is a "propitiation for the sins of the whole world," only those who appeal to this Propitiator actually escape condemnation under the divine law and are justified. The act of justification is not simultaneous with the atonement made by Christ.

---

7 German: Weiter wird gelehrt, daß wir Vergebung der Sünden und Gerechtigkeit vor Gott nicht erlangen mögen durch unser Verdienst, Werke und Genugtun, sondern daß wir Vergebung der Sünden bekommen und vor Gott gerecht werden aus Gnaden, um Christus' willen, durch den Glauben, 2] so wir glauben, daß Christus für uns gelitten hat und daß uns um seinetwillen die Sünden vergeben, Gerechtigkeit und ewiges Leben geschenkt wird.3] Denn diesen Glauben will Gott für Gerechtigkeit vor ihm halten und zurechnen, wie St. Paulus sagt zu den Römern am 3. und 4.
Latin: Item docent, quod homines non possint iustificari coram Deo propriis viribus, meritis aut operibus, sed gratis iustificentur propter 2] Christum per fidem, quum credunt se in gratiam recipi et peccata remitti propter Christum, qui sua morte pro nostris peccatis 3] satisfecit. Hanc fidem imputat Deus pro iustitia coram ipso, Rom. 3 et 4.

Fourth, since "the just requirement of the Law must be fulfilled in those who are to be justified," and since the only way in which that just requirement can be fulfilled for any sinner is if the accused pleads the "foreign righteousness" of Christ as his defense, then it would actually be *contrary* to God's justice for Him to absolve or acquit the guilty man who is *not* using the "foreign righteousness" of Christ as his defense before the judgment seat of God.

Fifth, Chemnitz says that his analogy presents the article of justification as clearly expressed by St. Paul in Romans 3. The burden is on those who wish to read an already-pronounced justification of all unbelievers into Romans 3:24 either to demonstrate how such an interpretation is compatible with Chemnitz' analogy, or admit that their own interpretation is at odds with Lutheran orthodoxy.

Sixth, note that Chemnitz refers this analogy to the "correct linguistic understanding of the word 'justification.'" He is not seeking to offer an arbitrary, partial or *ad hoc* definition of the word, but to faithfully convey the meaning of the word as used throughout the Holy Scripture. As he says elsewhere, "Our question is in what sense the Holy Spirit employs the word 'justify' in those passages of the Scripture in which He treats and teaches the doctrine of justification, as we have already shown it most clearly." (*Examination, Vol. 1*, 476)

Chemnitz' analogy illustrates that the concept of forensic justification, as described by the Lutheran Fathers, is not a piecemeal justification that already "happened" for all sinners, whether or not they appeal to the foreign righteousness of Christ, and then later "happens" again through the Word and faith. Instead, it is the culmination of the four "causes" that comprise the article of justification, each of which is a *sine qua non* in forensic justification. There can be no forensic justification of the sinner without God's grace, or without the merit of Christ, or without the sinner being clothed by faith in the foreign righteousness of Christ, or without the promise of the Gospel that kindles faith.

The Lutheran Fathers have much to say about the unique role that each of these four components plays in forensic justification.

The grace of God

The grace of God is sometimes spoken of by the Lutheran Fathers as the "efficient cause" of justification. The "efficient cause" is the "doer" of something, the person (or the thing) responsible for effecting something. Gerhard says that "the chief efficient cause is the grace of God, that is, God's free favor that takes our misery into account." Leyser names God Himself as the "efficient cause" of justification, while identifying God's grace as the "interior motivating cause." (See Appendix 1, Leyser)

The grace of God is behind every step of the sinner's justification. It was grace that moved God in eternity to make the decree that the human race, which would plunge itself into ruin, would be "redeemed and reconciled to God through Christ[8]." It was grace that moved God to send the Son of God into the world to offer His life as a sacrifice for the sins of His enemies. It is God's grace that moves God to permit sinners to plead the foreign righteousness of His Son. It is grace that moves God to send His Spirit and cause the Gospel to be preached in a hostile world, and it is grace that still moves God to kindle faith in the hearts of those who, by nature, despise God's grace, so that they may be received into grace and adopted as His children.

Without the grace of God, sinners would be abandoned to the tribunal of the Law as the only tribunal at which they could be judged. Their works have already been examined ac-

8 FC:SD:XI:15

cording to the Law and found wanting. Their condemnation before the Law has already been in place from the moment of their conception. But because God is rich in mercy, He "does not desire the death of anyone, but that all should come to repentance." Because of the abundance of the grace of God, who "wants all men to be saved and to come to a knowledge of the truth," He sent His Son to fulfill the Law's demands, to "satisfy" the Law vicariously, in the place of all sinners, and so to merit the setting up of this alternate place of judgment called the "Throne of Grace," or the "righteousness of faith."

The merit of Christ

The merit of Christ includes "the entire Christ according to both natures, in His obedience alone, which as God and man He rendered to the Father even unto death, and thereby merited for us the forgiveness of sins and eternal life.[9]" It refers to all the benefits that Christ has merited—*earned* and *deserved*—for the whole world of sinners by His perfect obedience to the Law and by His innocent sufferings and death. The merits of Christ (and often, Christ Himself[10]) are called "the price, or propitiation,[11]" that is, that which causes God to be favorable. Christ's obedience and death have made "satisfaction[12]" (also called "atonement" or "expiation[13]") to the demands of God's holy Law that required obedience from mankind, as well as the death and eternal condemnation of all who sin. Thus Christ has "merited" (or "won, achieved[14]," "acquired, obtained[15]") for all people the benefits of redemption, reconciliation, forgiveness of sins, remission of sins, righteousness,

9 FC:Ep:III:3
10 AC:XX:9, AC:XXI:2, Ap:III (Of Love):58, Ap:III:143
11 Ap:IV:53
12 AC:IV:2;Ap:IV:40; Ap:III(V):57
13 Ap:XXIV:23
14 AE:40:213
15 FC:Ep:V:5

eternal life, salvation, regeneration, adoption as God's children, an eternal inheritance, the giving of the Holy Spirit, renewal. Christ is said to have "redeemed" the human race in that He has paid the ransom price for the human race with His holy, precious blood. Christ is said to have "made reconciliation" for the human race by opening up a point of "access[16]" between sinners and God, namely, "in His blood."

The Formula of Concord summarizes it like this:

> But the Gospel is properly such a doctrine as teaches what man who has not observed the Law, and therefore is condemned by it, is to believe, namely, that Christ has expiated and made satisfaction for all sins, and has obtained and acquired for him, without any merit of his [no merit of the sinner intervening], forgiveness of sins, righteousness that avails before God, and eternal life. (FC:Ep:V:5)

Note here what man is to believe. First, that Christ has "expiated and made satisfaction for all sins." Second, that in so doing, Christ has obtained and acquired for him "forgiveness... righteousness...and eternal life."

Chemnitz:

> We have cited these testimonies to demonstrate that Christ alone has made satisfaction for all our sins, for guilt, and for punishment, so that there is nothing remaining for us to suffer or to make satisfaction for in expiating our sins. The passion of Christ and His being made a curse for us are substituted for our punishment, Gal. 3:13. The obedience of Christ is substituted for our guilt, for "He was made sin for us," 2 Cor. 5:21. We should carefully note this division of these points, Is. 53:6: "The sins of all were laid upon Him"; John 1:29: "He takes away the sins of the world"; Rom. 8:32; 1 John 2:2; Rom. 5:15; Titus 2:14. 2 Cor. 5:14: "If one died for all, then were all dead." (*Loci Theologici*, p. 550)

(See also Appendix 1, Leyser and Gerhard on the "mer-

---

16 Ap:IV:81

itorious cause" of justification.)

The "time" of the atonement made by Christ and the earning of benefits for the human race began with the conception and birth of the Son of God, who was "born under Law to redeem those under the Law" (Gal. 4:4-5), and was brought to completion or "finished" on the cross (John 19:30). Christ "made satisfaction for our sins" (AC:IV). And with regard to the scope of the atonement and the merit of Christ, the Lutheran Fathers readily acknowledged the universality of it and insisted in all their writings, especially against the Calvinist error, that Christ suffered and died for all.

Hunnius: "This notwithstanding, we most willingly grant that there is a righteousness that avails before God for the entire human race, a righteousness that has been gained and acquired through Christ" (*Theses Opposed to Huberianism,* Thesis 5 on Justification).

Hunnius in *A Clear Explanation of the Controversy among the Wittenberg Theologians Concerning Regeneration and Election* (pp. 7-8):

> Outside the controversy are these things:
>
> 1) That God seriously "wants all men to be saved and to come to a knowledge of the truth," 1 Tim. 2. We want this to be understood on both sides concerning the entire human race over against the blasphemies of the Calvinists, as also the rest of the Holy Spirit's testimonies say: "As I live, I do not desire the death of the wicked, but that the wicked turn and live" (Ezek. 33). "I do not desire the death of the one who dies" (Ezek. 18). "The Lord does not want anyone to perish, but that all should be turned back to repentance" (2 Pet. 3).
>
> 2) That God sent His Son for the whole world, and that the Son was made the propitiation not only for our sins, but also for the sins of the whole world, 1 John 2. And that He is the Lamb of God who takes away the sin of the world (John 1).

> Therefore, there never was nor will there be in the future any man for whose sins Christ did not shed His blood, to such an extent that the Scripture plainly affirms that His death was also for the reprobate and perishing (1 Cor. 8, 2 Pet. 2).
>
> 3) That the merit of the Son is seriously offered to all men. "Preach the Gospel to every creature" (Mark 16). "Now God commands men that all people everywhere should come to their senses" (Acts 17). "Turn to me and you will all be saved—all the ends of the earth" (Isaiah 45). "Come to me, all you who labor and are burdened" (Matt. 11).

Indeed, that Christ died for all is said to be the singular object of justifying faith.

> From that general faith that believes that Christ has suffered and died for the human race is born that special faith by which any believer says with the Apostle, *Christ loved me* (Gal. 2:20). Therefore, he does not doubt that the benefits of Christ pertain also to him and that they are offered to him in the word of the Gospel, and consequently he applies them to himself in hope. From this special application of the benefits of Christ is born that "access to God." (Gerhard, *Adnotationes*, Rom. 5:2, translation mine)

The resurrection of Christ is also said to be the object of justifying faith in this sense:

> *One asks, why is Christ's resurrection from the dead declared specifically to be the object of justifying faith?* We reply: (1) Because by raising His Son, our bondsman, who was put to death for our sins, God made manifest by that very act that full satisfaction has been made to Him by His death. (2) Consideration is given at the same time to the power of God which He exerted in the raising of Christ (Eph. 1:20). This is how that statement is applied to the example of Abraham, whose faith is commended in 4:20 for the fact that *he gave praise to God*. (3) The summary of the entire Gospel is contained in this article of the resurrection of Christ, and this single article encompasses all the rest (1 Cor. 15:1 ff.). For it is understood from the fact that Christ rose from the dead

> that He truly died. And since He truly died, He was therefore also truly conceived and born, and truly suffered for our sins. (Gerhard, *Adnotationes*, Rom. 4:24, translation mine)

Without the grace of God and the merit of Christ, sinners would have no righteousness to plead before God, no sacrifice to hold up before God, no Mediator, no Propitiator or Reconciler, no Throne of Grace. They would, again, be left appealing only to the Law. But since the merit of Christ is in place, since "the work of redemption is done and accomplished" and "Christ has acquired and gained the treasure for us by His suffering, death, resurrection, and so on," there is indeed a Righteous One to whom sinners can flee for refuge in God's judgment.

Faith

But neither the grace of God nor the merit of Christ, without this "fleeing for refuge," results in the justification of sinners. That Christ has earned or acquired the benefits of forgiveness, life, salvation, righteousness and adoption for someone, is not the same thing as saying that a person (much less the entire world) has already been "forgiven" or "made alive" or "saved" or "declared righteous" or "adopted." As Chemnitz explained in his courtroom analogy, Christ with His merit stands as a Throne of Grace to which all sinners are invited to appeal. But the merits of Christ do not benefit the sinner in the courtroom without such an appeal, because the merits of Christ must be applied or "counted" or "credited" to the sinner. The merit of Christ is applied to sinners through ***imputation,*** and imputation takes place ***by faith***. Faith may be called "using Christ as a Mediator."

Numerous testimonies from the Lutheran Fathers can be adduced.

> Now we will show that faith justifies ‹and nothing else›.

> Here, in the first place, readers must be taught about this point: Just as it is necessary to keep this statement—Christ is Mediator—so is it necessary to defend that faith justifies. For how will Christ be Mediator if we do not use Him as Mediator in justification, if we do not hold that we are counted righteous for His sake? To believe is to trust in Christ's merits, that for His sake God certainly wishes to be reconciled with us. Here is a similar point: Just as we should defend that the promise of Christ is necessary apart from the Law, so also we should defend that faith justifies. (Ap:IV:69-70)
>
> But in justification we have to treat with God; His wrath must be appeased and conscience must be pacified with respect to God. None of these occur through the works of the Second Table [by love, but only by faith, which apprehends Christ and the promise of God. (Ap:V:103)

The entire third article of the Solid Declaration portrays the justification of the sinner in these terms, in perfect harmony with Chemnitz' courtroom analogy. A few sections will be cited here.

> We unanimously believe, teach, and confess the following about the righteousness of faith before God, in accordance with the comprehensive summary of our faith and confession presented above. A poor sinful person is justified before God, that is, absolved and declared free and exempt from all his sins and from the sentence of well-deserved condemnation, and is adopted into sonship and inheritance of eternal life, without any merit or worth of his own. This happens without any preceding, present, or subsequent works, out of pure grace, because of the sole merit, complete obedience, bitter suffering, death, and resurrection of our Lord Christ alone. His obedience is credited to us for righteousness.
>
> These treasures are brought to us by the Holy Spirit in the promise of the Holy Gospel. Faith alone is the only means through which we lay hold on, accept, apply, and take them for ourselves. This faith is God's gift [Ephesians 2:8–9], by

which we truly learn to know Christ, our Redeemer, in the Word of the Gospel and trust in Him. We trust that for the sake of His obedience alone we have the forgiveness of sins by grace, are regarded as godly and righteous by God the Father, and are eternally saved. Therefore, it is considered and understood to be the same thing when Paul says (a) we are "justified by faith" (Romans 3:28) or (b) "faith is counted as righteousness" (Romans 4:5) and when he says (c) "by the one man's obedience the many will be made righteous" (Romans 5:19) or (d) "so one act of righteousness leads to justification and life for all men" (Romans 5:18). Faith justifies not because it is such a good work or because it is so beautiful a virtue. It justifies because it lays hold of and accepts Christ's merit in the promise of the Holy Gospel. For this merit must be applied and become ours through faith, if we are to be justified by it. Therefore, the righteousness that is credited to faith or to the believer out of pure grace is Christ's obedience, suffering, and resurrection, since He has made satisfaction for us to the Law and paid for ‹expiated› our sins. (FC:SD:III:9-14)

This righteousness [of Christ] is offered us by the Holy Ghost through the Gospel and in the Sacraments, and is applied, appropriated, and received through faith, whence believers have reconciliation with God, forgiveness of sins, the grace of God sonship, and heirship of eternal life. Accordingly, the word justify here means to declare righteous and free from sins, and to absolve one from eternal punishment for the sake of Christ's righteousness, which is imputed by God to faith, Phil. 3, 9. For this use and understanding of this word is common in the Holy Scriptures of the Old and the New Testament. (FC:SD:III:16-17)

This remains the office and property of faith alone. It alone, and nothing else, is the means or instrument with and through which God's grace and Christ's merit in the Gospel promise are received, apprehended, accepted, applied to us, and appropriated. (FC:SD:III:38)

Chemnitz describes in detail in his *Examination* and

Loci that justification is the end result of the application of the merit of Christ, which is made by imputation of the righteousness of Christ to believers. This section from his *Enchiridion* also states the matter concisely:

> ***145 In What, Then, Does Justification of Man the Sinner Before God Consist According to the Statement of the Gospel?***
>
> In this very thing, that God imputes to us the righteousness of the obedience and death of Christ the Mediator and thus justifies us freely out of grace, without our works or merits, alone by faith that apprehends the grace of God the Father and the merit of Christ; that is, He forgives us [our] sins, receives [us] into grace, adopts [us] as [His] sons, and receives [us] to the inheritance of life eternal. Ro 4:24–25, 28; 4:5; 10:4; Gl 3:24; Eph 2:8–9; Tts 3:5–7.
>
> ***149 Are All Men Justified and Saved Because of This Righteousness of the Son of God?***
>
> The way is broad that leads to damnation, and there are many that walk in it. Mt 7:13.
>
> ***150 What, Then is the Reason? Did Christ Not Make Satisfaction for All? or Does the Heavenly Father Not Want This Benefit to Be Common to All?***
>
> The cause or fault of damnation is by no means to be ascribed to God. For Christ is the propitiation for the sins of the whole world, 1 Jn 2:2. And the will of God is that no one should perish, but that all be saved. 1 Ti 2:4; 2 Ptr 3:9; Eze 18:23; Mt 18:14. But it is by the fault of men that not all are saved, because not all accept that benefit. Jn 1:5, 10–11; 3:19. For it is necessary that the benefit or merit of Christ become ours (Ro 8:32), that is, that it be applied to us, so that each one accept and apprehend it (Jn 1:12), and thus Christ be in us (Jn 6:56) and we be found in Him (Ph 3:8–9).
>
> ***151 By What Means is Christ, or the Merit of Christ, Applied to Us?***

For that application two things are absolutely required: First, that God, through the Holy Spirit set forth, offer, present, and give to us that benefit. For this purpose God has established a certain means or instrument, namely the word of the Gospel and the Sacraments. That means is, as it were, the hand of God, which He extends and opens to us, offering and presenting to us the merit and benefits of His Son for our salvation. Ro 10:17; 2 Co 5:19–20; Tts 3:5.

The other thing that is required for application is that we apprehend, receive, and apply to ourselves the benefit of the sons of God that is offered and presented to us in the Word and the Sacraments; this is done by no other means or instruments than faith. Ro 1:17; 3:28; 4:5; Jn 3:15–16; Gl 3:22, 24. For faith is, as it were, our hand with which we take, apprehend, and accept the benefits of Christ. Jn 1:12. And it is a kind of bond by which we are bound to Christ, that He might be and dwell in us (Eph 3:17) and that we might be found in Him (Ph 3:8–9).

Hunnius teaches the same thing:

We interpret those things that the Scripture contains regarding the redemption and reconciliation of the world (or of the human race) concerning the benefit gained and acquired through the death of Christ, and concerning the sufficiency of that merit of Christ—that it is sufficient for the whole world to be reconciled, justified and saved, if the whole world were to believe; that it was also intended for the world and acquired to this end, that all men should thence obtain salvation through faith. Meanwhile, God has never intended it to mean that it avails for justifying or for remitting sins without faith, through some sort of general remission of sins or justification, which is also supposedly done among those who never have faith, never had faith, or never will have faith. He who does not believe, says John the Baptist, will not see life, but the wrath of God remains on him (John 3). Therefore, regarding those who never believe in the Son of God, from them also the wrath of God was never withdrawn (not even for a moment). However much

> the treasure of the expiation of sins has been obtained for them and offered to them in the Gospel, nevertheless, it was never conferred on them through unbelief, nor was it ever received by them, since faith was lacking to them, which is the only organ for receiving the remission of sins. (*A Clear Explanation,* p. 60).

Hunnius concludes, as did Chemnitz, that it would be contrary to God's justice to justify anyone who is *not* clothed by faith in the foreign righteousness of Christ:

> But Proverbs 17 says that it is an abomination before God if someone justifies an ungodly man. Knowing this, how, then, shall we attribute this to God Himself?
>
> There is a great difference between the two. To be sure, in a human judgment (where the imputation of a foreign righteousness has no place), it is called "justifying the ungodly" when he who is neither righteous by his own nor by a foreign righteousness is reckoned and pronounced righteous, without respect to or intervention of any righteousness—that is, by a false and unjust sentence. But in God's judgment, where a foreign righteousness is valid, the ungodly is justified, not without any righteousness at all, but, since he lacks his own righteousness (and is for this very reason "ungodly" by nature), nonetheless, he is clothed by faith with a foreign righteousness which most certainly can be and is imputed to believers by God, as was just demonstrated. (*Articulus de Justificatione,* p. 67, translation mine.)

Polycarp Leyser describes the role of faith as a "cause of application" in embracing the treasures of God hidden in Christ (see Appendix 1) and concludes: "And since no works of the Law, neither preceding nor present nor subsequent, constitute any cause (either of merit or of application), therefore we rightly and piously declare that *man is justified by faith alone in Christ.*"

Gerhard likewise insists, in *Adnotationes* on Rom. 3:26, that "The object of justification is man the sinner, but only such a one as believes in Christ, that is, who acknowledges his sins from the Law, who seriously grieves over them, and who by faith applies to himself the promise of the remission of sins for the sake of Christ" (translation mine).

He then answers the following question in discussing Romans 5:18, taking it for granted that everyone knows that "not all men are justified":

> *But how did the righteousness of Christ overflow to all men for justification, since not all men are justified?* We reply: The Apostle is not talking about the application of the benefit, but about the acquisition of the benefit. If we want to descend to the application, that universality must be restricted to those who are grafted into Christ by faith. For as the unrighteousness of Adam is communicated to all those who are descended from him by carnal generation, so the righteousness of Christ is communicated to all those who are grafted into Him through faith and spiritual regeneration (translation mine).

(See also Appendix 2, Gerhard on Romans 5:18)

Luther draws the same conclusion in his Galatians commentary. Throughout he assumes the same outline that Chemnitz expressed in his analogy. There is a Throne of Grace to which all sinners are invited to flee. But only those who flee to Him in faith (that is, those who are "in Him" by faith[17]), and thus receive the application of His merit, are justified. A few examples are cited here. (See Appendix 3 for more citations from Luther's Galatians commentary.)

> [Paraphrasing the Apostle Paul:] "Therefore my doctrine is true, pure, sure, and divine. Nor can there be any

---

17 Luther: "The question is what Christ is and what blessing He has brought us. Christ is not the Law; He is not my work or that of the Law; He is not my love or that of the Law; He is not my chastity, obedience, or poverty. But He is the Lord of life and death, the Mediator and Savior of sinners, the Redeemer of those who are under the Law. **By faith we are in Him, and He is in us** (John 6:56)." (*Luther's Works, Vol. 26*, 137)

doctrine that is different from mine, much less better. Therefore any doctrine at all that does not teach as mine does—that all men are sinners and are justified solely by faith in Christ—must be false, uncertain, evil, blasphemous, accursed, and demonic. And so are those who either teach or accept such a doctrine." (*Luther's works, vol. 26*: *Lectures on Galatians*, 59)

Therefore faith justifies because it takes hold of and possesses this treasure, the present Christ. But how He is present—this is beyond our thought; for there is darkness, as I have said. Where the confidence of the heart is present, therefore, there Christ is present, in that very cloud and faith. This is the formal righteousness on account of which a man is justified; it is not on account of love, as the sophists say. In short, just as the sophists say that love forms and trains faith, so we say that it is Christ who forms and trains faith or who is the form of faith. Therefore the Christ who is grasped by faith and who lives in the heart is the true Christian righteousness, on account of which God counts us righteous and grants us eternal life. (*Luther's works, vol. 26*, 59)

Here it is to be noted that these three things are joined together: faith, Christ, and acceptance or imputation. Faith takes hold of Christ and has Him present, enclosing Him as the ring encloses the gem. And whoever is found having this faith in the Christ who is grasped in the heart, him God accounts as righteous. This is the means and the merit by which we obtain the forgiveness of sins and righteousness. "Because you believe in Me," God says, "and your faith takes hold of Christ, whom I have freely given to you as your Justifier and Savior, therefore be righteous." Thus God accepts you or accounts you righteous only on account of Christ, in whom you believe. (*Luther's works, vol. 26*, 132)

This does not mean that there is no sin in us, as the sophists have taught when they said that we must go on doing good until we are no longer conscious of any sin; but sin is always present, and the godly feel it. But it is ignored and hidden in the sight of God, because Christ the Mediator stands between; because we take hold of Him by faith, all our sins are sins no longer. But where Christ and faith are not present, here there is no forgiveness of sins or hiding of sins. On the contrary, here there is the sheer imputation and condemnation of sins. Thus God wants to glorify His Son, and He Himself wants to be glorified in us through Him. (*Luther's works, vol. 26*, 133)

But the true theology teaches that there is no more sin in the world, because Christ, on whom, according to Is. 53:6, the Father has laid the sins of the entire world, has conquered, destroyed, and killed it in His own body. Having died to sin once, He has truly been raised from the dead and will not die any more (Rom. 6:9). Therefore wherever there is faith in Christ, there sin has in fact been abolished, put to death, and buried. But where there is no faith in Christ, there sin remains. And although there are still remnants of sin in the saints because they do not believe perfectly, nevertheless these remnants are dead; for on account of faith in Christ they are not imputed. (*Luther's works, vol. 26*, 286)[18]

Luther also writes in his *Bondage of the Will*:

This pair of statements by Paul, that "the righteous lives by faith" (Rom. 1:17), and that "whatsoever is not of faith, is sin" (Rom. 14:23), stand confirmed. The latter follows from the former; for if it is only by faith that we are justified, it is evident that they who are without faith are not yet justified; and those who are not justified are sinners; and sinners are evil trees, and can only sin and bear evil fruit (*The Bondage of the Will*, 301).

---

18 Those who wish to ascribe a "universal justification" to Luther based on the first sentence of this paragraph would do well to read it all the way to the end of the paragraph. Luther commonly makes broad statements like this that he goes on to explain later. To cite another example: "Now that Christ reigns, ***there is in fact no more sin, death, or curse***—this we confess every day in the Apostles' Creed when we say: "I believe in the holy church." This is plainly nothing else than if we were to say: "I believe that there is no sin and no death ***in the church.*** For believers in Christ are not sinners and are not sentenced to death but are altogether holy and righteous, lords over sin and death who live eternally." (*Luther's Works, Vol. 26*, 285)

Without faith, by which a sinner flees to the Throne of Grace for mercy and through which the foreign righteousness of Christ is imputed, the sinner remains in his natural-born condition of appealing to the Law. But all who seek to be justified by works of the Law stand condemned before God, not justified, not absolved, not declared righteous. There are only two possibilities. A person is either appealing to the Law in unbelief or he is appealing in faith to the Throne of Grace for mercy. The former stands condemned before God, not justified; the latter stands justified before God, not condemned.

The Promise of the Gospel

But faith is an utter impossibility for sinners, who are, by nature, hostile to God, blind to spiritual things and dead in sins and transgressions. No one can know about the mercy of God or the Throne of Grace by nature, and even after learning about its existence, no one would want it, no one would flee to it willingly, except for ***the promise of the Gospel.***

> That we may obtain this faith, the Ministry of Teaching the Gospel and administering the Sacraments was instituted. For through the Word and Sacraments, as through instruments, 2] the Holy Ghost is given, who works faith; where and when it pleases God, in them that hear 3] the Gospel, to wit, that God, not for our own merits, but for Christ's sake, justifies those who believe that they are received into grace for Christ's sake. (AC:V)

The Holy Spirit, working through the means of grace, is the Person of the Holy Trinity who "gives to the unbelievers the gift of faith, and makes willing men out of those that were unwilling,[19]" as St. Augustine says, so that believers are justified in the divine courtroom. Hence Polycarp Leyser can

19 Augustine of Hippo. P. Schaff (Ed.), *A Select Library of the Nicene and Post-Nicene Fathers of the Christian Church, First Series, Volume V: Saint Augustin: Anti-Pelagian Writings*, 549.

refer to the entire Holy Trinity as the "efficient cause" or the "doer" of justification, because sinners are not justified by the Father's work alone, nor by the Son's work alone, but by the combined working of Father, Son and Holy Spirit. "The efficient cause of justification is the entire Holy Trinity. For the Father justifies us, in His Son, our Lord Jesus Christ, through the Holy Spirit (1 Cor. 6)" (*De Iustificatione Hominis,* Proposition 1, par. 4, translation mine. See also Appendix 1).

This is also the reason why the article on the forgiveness of sins is treated in the Third Article of the Apostles Creed (not to mention the Nicene Creed, which confesses "one Baptism for the remission of sins"). It is not that forgiveness is earned for us as the Holy Spirit works through Word and Sacrament, even as ministers do not pronounce absolution by saying, "I make atonement for your sins." Atonement *was* made; the earning *was* accomplished at the cross. Absolution *is* pronounced; the merit *is* applied through the ministry of the Word. It is through the application of what Christ has earned that sinners are actually forgiven, absolved and acquitted, so that justification "happens" through the Word:

> God cannot be interacted with, God cannot be grasped, except through the Word. So justification happens through the Word, just as Paul says in Romans 1:16, '[The Gospel] is the power of God for salvation to everyone who believes.' Likewise, he says in 10:17, 'Faith comes from hearing.' Proof can be derived even from this: faith justifies because, if justification happens only through the Word, and the Word is understood only by faith, it follows that faith justifies. (Ap:IV:67)

What, then, is "the Gospel" through which the Holy Spirit applies the righteousness of Christ to sinners? It is a promise, a promise that God will do something, namely, that He will "save everyone who believes." The promise, to refer back to Chemnitz' analogy, is not, "Everyone in the world has already been absolved." The promise is not, "Everyone in the world has already been declared righteous." That is neither true, nor is it a promise. The promise of the Gospel, rather, is that the poor sinner who flees for refuge to the Throne of Grace receives forgiveness, is absolved, is justified, is received into God's grace and eternal life for the sake of the merit of Christ. The promise is that Christ's righteousness affords a dependable shelter from the accusations of the law, so that "he who believes on Him will by no means be put to shame" (1 Pet. 2:6). The promise is that, although mercy is found nowhere else in the universe, it will surely be found at the Throne of Grace.

The Apology states: "And, again, as often as we speak of faith, we wish an object to be understood, namely, the promised mercy. For faith justifies and saves, not on the ground that it is a work in itself worthy, but only because it receives the promised mercy" (Ap:IV:55-56). And again, "Christ Himself, since He has appeared, promises the remission of sins, justification, and life eternal" (Ap:IV:5).

Chemnitz summarizes it as follows: "The Gospel (as the Apology says) is properly the promise of remission of sins and of justification for the sake of Christ, preaching the righteousness of faith in Christ" (*Enchiridion,* 69). And in this longer section from the *Enchiridion:*

> ***136 What are the Chief Parts in Which the Doctrine of the Gospel is Comprehended and Set Forth?***
>
> The Gospel is properly the doctrine of the person and office or benefits of Christ. But this doctrine consists most of all in these chief parts:
>
> I. That the Son of God, before the world of time, was, by a wonderful decree made in the hidden counsel of the Trinity, appointed to be our Mediator, Redeemer, Reconciler, and Savior.
>
> II. That this decree was revealed by the word of promise immediately after the Fall, and the promise of the com-

ing Messiah gradually renewed and repeated to the fathers during the whole time of the Old Testament.

III. Likewise that the Son of God, according to the promise, was made man in the fullness of time and most perfectly completed the work of redemption and reconciliation by His obedience, passion, and death, and thus gained righteousness and life eternal, by His resurrection and ascension, for those who believe in Him.

IV. The Gospel does not only set forth the account of Christ in story form, but the proper doctrine of Him is the promise of grace, by which God, in the Word and the Sacraments, sets before and offers to miserable sinners—thoroughly terrified by the knowledge of sins and of divine wrath and damnation—grace, remission of sins, adoption, and the inheritance of life eternal freely and out of pure mercy or grace, without our merit, only for the sake of the obedience, passion, death, and merit of Christ.

V. The Gospel teaches that these benefits of Christ the Mediator are to be apprehended and applied by faith.

VI. The Gospel declares those who believe righteous and saved.

The Gospel tells about the goodness and mercy of Christ, and that He helps all who come to Him for help. This is how Luther most often speaks in his sermons, describing how people came to Jesus with their maladies and diseases because they had heard the "good report" about Christ. This believing the good report about Christ is already identified by Luther as "faith."

Now this confidence of faith or knowledge of the goodness of Christ would never have originated in this leper by virtue of his own reason, if he had not first heard a good report about Christ, namely, how kind, gracious and merciful he is, ready to help and befriend, comfort and counsel every one that comes to him. Such a report must undoubtedly have come to his ears, and from this fame he derived

> courage, and turned and interpreted the report to his own advantage. He applied this goodness to his own need and concluded with all confidence: To me also he will be as kind as his fame and good report declare. His faith therefore did not grow out of his reason, but out of the report he heard of Christ, as St. Paul says: "Belief cometh of hearing, and hearing by the Word (or report) of Christ." Rom 10, 17. (*Luther's Sermons, Volume 2*. "Sermon for Third Sunday after Epiphany, Matthew 8:1-13.")

But what does it look like in practice? Where is Christ to be found, now that He is ascended into heaven? Where is the Throne of Grace located and how are sinners to flee to it for mercy?

The Throne of Grace is not to be sought in heaven. Rather, it is to be sought in the Church, where "the Gospel is rightly taught and the Sacraments are rightly administered." (AC:VII) So Luther can say in the Large Catechism, "For we are in the Christian Church, where there is nothing but continuous, uninterrupted forgiveness of sin. This is because God forgives us and because we forgive, bear with, and help one another. But outside of this Christian Church, where the Gospel is not found, there is no forgiveness, as also there can be no holiness" (Creed, Third Article, par. 55).

How does one flee for refuge to the Throne of Grace? One flees for refuge, first, to Holy Baptism where the Throne of Grace is to be found. This is where the Apostle Peter told the convicted crowds on the Day of Pentecost to flee: "Repent, and let every one of you be baptized in the name of Jesus Christ for the remission of sins" (Acts 2:38). It is in Holy Baptism that sinners are "buried with Christ into death" and raised to new life and new birth. It is for good reason that the Book of Concord so often equates "remission of sins" and "justification" with "regeneration"[20] and locates them both in Baptism:

---

20 Ap:XIIb:60: "...We attribute justification and regeneration to this faith." FC:SD:III:18: "The word regeneration is sometimes used for the word justification." Et al.

What does Baptism give or profit? —Answer: It works forgiveness of sins, delivers from death and the devil, and gives eternal salvation to all who believe this, as the words and promises of God declare. (Small Catechism: Baptism Second)

Augustine speaks in the same way when he says, "Sin is forgiven in Baptism, not in such a way that it no longer exists, but so that it is not charged." (Ap:II:36)

And on this account let no one boast of works, because no one is justified by his deeds. But he who is righteous has it given him because he was justified after the laver [of Baptism]. Faith, therefore, is that which frees through the blood of Christ, because he is blessed "whose transgression is forgiven, whose sin is covered," Ps. 32, 1. These are the words of Ambrose, which clearly favor our doctrine; he denies justification to works, and ascribes to faith that it sets us free through the blood of Christ. (Ap:IV:103-105)

Luther offers this vivid picture in one of his sermons:

Likewise in the last chapter of his epistle he says of Christ, "This is he who came by water and blood, Jesus Christ, not with the water only but with the water and the blood" [I John 5:6]. Thus he is always wanting to mingle the blood in the baptism in order that we may see in it the innocent, rosy-red blood of Christ. For human eyes, it is true, there appears to be nothing there but pure white water, but St. John wants us to open the inward and spiritual eyes of faith in order that we may see, not only water, but also the blood of our Lord Jesus Christ.

Why? Because this holy baptism was purchased for us through this same blood, which he shed for us and with which he paid for sin. This blood and its merit and power he put into baptism, in order that in baptism we might receive it. For whenever a person receives baptism in faith this is the same as if he were visibly washed and cleansed of sin with the blood of Christ. For we do not attain the forgiveness of sins through our work, but rather through the death

> and the shedding of the blood of the Son of God. But he takes this forgiveness of sin and tucks it into baptism. (*Luther's Works, Vol. 51*, 325)

Gerhard, too, sends the troubled sinner back to his Baptism:

> Therefore, if you are baptized, you can by no means doubt that you have the grace of God, remission of sins, and the promise of eternal life. Where there is regeneration, there is remission of sins, the grace of God, perfect righteousness, renewal, the gift of the Holy Spirit, adoption, and the inheritance of eternal life." (*Handbook of Consolations*, 30).

One flees for refuge to the Throne of Grace in the Sacrament of the Altar, where He finds Christ handing out, together with His very body and blood, forgiveness of sins, life and salvation.

> *What is the benefit of such eating and drinking?*—Answer. That is shown us in these words: Given, and shed for you, for the remission of sins; namely, that in the Sacrament forgiveness of sins, life, and salvation are given us through these words. For where there is forgiveness of sins, there is also life and salvation. (Small Catechism: Sacrament of the Altar)

> In the second place, there is besides this command also a promise, as we heard above, which ought most strongly to incite and encourage us. For here stand the kind and precious words: This is My body, given for you. This is My blood, shed for you, for the remission of sins...For here He offers to us the entire treasure which He has brought for us from heaven, and to which He invites us also in other places with the greatest kindness, as when He says in St. Matthew 11, 28: Come unto Me, all ye that labor and are heavy laden, and I will give you rest. (LC:Sacrament of the Altar:64,66)

Finally, one flees for refuge to the Throne of Grace in Holy Absolution, where the sentence is delivered from the

Throne of Grace through the mouth of the pastor, as penitent sinners "flee for refuge to Thine infinite mercy, seeking and imploring Thy grace for the sake of our Lord Jesus Christ..."[21] As Gerhard urges:

> *DOUBT CONCERNING THE APPLICATION OF THE MERIT OF CHRIST*
>
> *TEMPTED.* Yes, of course, it is stated plainly that the merit of Christ is universal, but, at the same time, I do not see that the benefit of Christ has been offered and applied to me in particular or individually. Many things are offered universally that nevertheless do not extend to the individual.
>
> *COMFORTER.* No! The species is rightly taken from the genus; it rightly proceeds from the universal to the particular. As such, because God desires all to be saved, you may rightly and most firmly believe that He wants you to be saved. Because it is said that Christ died for all, you may rightly and most firmly believe that He died on the Cross for you and He wants to cleanse you from all your sins by His own blood. Moreover, what is offered by the Word of the Gospel for all in general is offered, presented, and applied by the Word of absolution to you in particular. Indeed, when the pastor of your church announces the remission of your sins in the name of God, you are to be certain that it is so established in heaven before God. This is how Christ arranged the matter: whatever you loose on earth shall be loosed in heaven (Matt 18:18) and anyone's sins you forgive, they are forgiven for that person (John 20:23). This is that salutary ministry of reconciliation (2 Cor 5:18) that God has entrusted to the pastors of the Church. These are the salutary keys that He committed to them in good faith. This is the salutary office of ambassadors that they perform in the name of Christ and by which God exhorts us and, as it were, implores us through them. What therefore is offered to you in particular, you must not doubt that it pertains to you in particular.
>
> When your heart is gravely distressed and you hear the voice of the pastor announcing the remission of sins in the

---

21 *The Lutheran Hymnal*, The Confession of Sins, p. 6

name of Christ, know that you have heard Christ Himself. Whatever the pastor does in the name of Christ before you, Christ Himself does. It is Christ who announces the remission of sins to you. The pastor, in his own voice, speaks on behalf of Christ. If uncertainty wants to creep into your heart concerning this, listen carefully to the words of Christ saying to the Apostles and their successors, He that hears you, hears me (Luke 10:16). It is not you that speak, but the Spirit of my Father (Matt 10:20). Listen to the words of John the Baptist, I am the voice of one crying (John 1:23). Truly I tell you, it is another that preaches and cries by me. The office is mine but the force and benefit of the office depends on another. Listen to the words of the Apostle, We are ambassadors for Christ (2 Cor 5:20). That is, in Christ's name and stead, as though God exhorts you by us. We pray on behalf of Christ that you be reconciled to God (2 Cor 5:20). Therefore he who despises this, despises not man but God, who gives to us His Holy Spirit (1 Thess 4:8).

> Believe, therefore, that even now, indeed today, Christ says to you as He did once to the paralytic and to the woman who was a sinner, Your sins are forgiven (Matt 9:2; Luke 7:48). There is, of course, no difference between these words of absolution and those uttered by the pastor; it matters not that one is spoken by man and the other by Christ. Therefore, when you hear the pastor announce to you the remission of sins, do not think that it is the voice of the pastor you hear but know that it is the voice of Christ. (Gerhard, *Handbook of Consolations*, 26-27).

And so the old outline remains intact for the Lutheran Church throughout the age of orthodoxy, from Luther to Gerhard. Justification is the result of (1) the grace of God who sent Christ to save the world and wants all men to be saved; (2) the merit of Christ, who was obedient for all, suffered and died for all, and made atonement for all; (3) faith that lays hold of the merit of Christ and through which the righteousness of Christ is imputed to sinners; and (4) the promise of the Gospel, in Word and Sacrament, that kindles and sustains faith, and furnishes for sinners a place on earth where the Throne of Grace is to be found.

Huber's Deviation from the Common Outline

This common outline, this "justification by faith alone in Christ" was the only concept of justification espoused by the Lutherans in the age of orthodoxy. No other justification was known in the Lutheran Church—until Samuel Huber (1547-1624) arrived on the scene.

Huber was brought to Wittenberg from Switzerland, via Tübingen, in 1592. In 1590, while still in Tübingen, Huber, fighting against the Calvinists, wrote a book comprised of 1185 theses entitled, "That Christ Jesus died for the sins of all men." This orthodox title and Huber's steadfast confession against the Calvinists of the universal atonement made by Christ served to convince the Lutheran theologians in Wittenberg that Huber would be a staunch ally as they sought to rid the German lands of Calvinism in all of its forms.

But within three years, the Wittenberg faculty noticed that Huber was straying from the "common (and Scriptural) outline" of justification. He was teaching a justification that "happened" for all men apart from the Word and apart from faith. It was a "general justification," a "universal justification" that was supposedly pronounced at some time on all men. As they dug back into his book of 1185 theses, the Wittenberg theologians found that he had already been teaching this false doctrine there.

> Our Churches have always taught and still teach the justification that is by faith and that pertains to believers, but that by no means extends to the whole world.
>
> Besides this justification by faith, Dr. Huber teaches some other justification that is equally common to the entire human race.

...Hence he writes in his Tübingen Theses, Thesis 270: "Moreover, this is the status and the condition of our redemption, that sins have been forgiven to all men equally, since the handwriting that was against us has been blotted out (Col. 2). Theses 59 & 60: "But meanwhile, no less truly, properly, actually and effectively has Christ conferred redemption on the entire human race—just as truly, properly, actually and effectively as Adam brought ruin upon each and every man. And lest anything remain in doubt, we are saying that, by the death and satisfaction of Christ for our sins, all judgment and divine wrath upon all men has been rightly, truly and properly removed and blotted out."

From these and many other examples from his own published books and writings, we are unable to come to any other conclusion but that Dr. Huber is clearly persuaded that, at some time (whether in eternity, or when God made the first promise in Paradise, or when Christ was sacrificed on the altar of the cross), the entire human race was—was, I say!— for the sake of the merit of Christ, truly received into grace, into the bosom and embrace of God; and that all men were loved in the Beloved through some general adoption; and that, through a justification that is just as general and extends just as widely as the condemnation from Adam extends widely upon all men equally, sins were forgiven to all men equally through a general remission of sins ; redemption was conferred on the entire human race in that very act and deed; and Adam's guilt has been truly and properly washed away in all men, so much so that all judgment and wrath of God has been removed and blotted out in all men—truly and properly. These are Huber's own words, faithfully transcribed from his books...

Here one may ask Dr. Huber when he thinks all this took place. When were all sins remitted equally to the entire human race? He has to confess one or the other—that this took place either from eternity, or in time. But it will be clearly demonstrated shortly that neither of these options can be true.

> In addition, since this general justification, according to Dr. Huber's hypothesis, embraces also unbelievers, let him respond to this: Were sins forgiven to them through the imputation of the obedience of Christ, or apart from it? If it was without the imputation of the obedience of Christ, then the eternal justice of God will be endangered, since He remits sins without regard for a mediating satisfaction. But if it is through the imputation of the merit of Christ, then let him explain: Does the Scripture ever, anywhere, mention any bare, simple imputation that is considered without respect to faith? And what need is there for several, since the Apostle teaches one method and one way alone for obtaining remission of sins, and that is through faith, so that he exclaims that, "We are not justified except through faith in Jesus Christ" (Gal. 2). There are a great many sermons on the justification of men before God in our published writings—in the Augsburg Confession, the Apology, the Smalcald Articles, in both Catechisms of Luther, in the Epitome and the Formula of Concord—indeed, in the entire controversy with the papists that has gone on now for more than 70 years. But regarding this general justification by which all men were supposedly justified at some time, received into the embrace of divine grace, adopted, with sin having been forgiven to all men equally—truly, properly and by the deed itself—of this, I say, in all of these published writings and in all of Holy Scripture, there is nothing but eternal silence. (Hunnius, *A Clear Explanation,* 57-62)

It can easily be determined, both from Huber's writings (especially his Tübingen Theses) and from Hunnius' writings against him, that Huber was by no means a "Universalist" in the modern sense of the word; he did not teach that all people go to heaven. Nor did Hunnius ever bring that accusation against him. In fact, Hunnius expressly states that Huber denied teaching such a thing[22]. What Huber did teach

22 Theses 12 & 13 on Election: "In addition, whether all men are, in fact, saved, including those who do not believe in Christ. This, likewise, is not, at the moment, being called into question. For although that conclusion can most definitely be reached from Huber's doctrine as a consequence

was that, although God had justified the whole world, people could reject this general justification and fall back under God's condemnation. But he taught that baptismal regeneration was necessary for salvation. He also taught that justification by faith was necessary for a person to be eternally saved.

Huber's problem was not that he was a Universalist. It was that he strayed from proper Biblical exegesis of certain passages, including Romans 5:12-20 (See Appendix 2, Hunnius on Romans 5:18). It was that he strayed from the common outline of forensic justification that requires the imputation, by faith, of Christ's righteousness in order for any sinner to be justified. It was that he strayed from the confessional Lutheran teaching that "restricts justification to believers only, as prescribed by all prophetic and apostolic Scriptures" (Hunnius, *Theses Opposed to Huberianism*, Thesis 20 Concerning Justification).

Conclusion

In conclusion, though much has been written, what was said in the introduction holds true. The article of justification, as taught in Scripture and in the Lutheran age of orthodoxy, can be fully grasped and appreciated with a statement as simple as John 3:16-18.

"For God so loved the world that He gave His only begotten Son, that whoever believes in Him should not perish but have everlasting life. For God did not send His Son into the world to condemn the world, but that the world through Him might be saved. He who believes in Him is not condemned; but he who does not

affirmed by the testimonies of Christ and the apostles, nevertheless, since Huber directly and intentionally does not teach in such a way, we are still willing not to charge him directly with that paradox." (Hunnius, *Theses Opposed to Huberianism,* Concerning Justification). This "paradox" of Huber's was that all men have been forgiven and justified before God, and yet not all men are saved. Hunnius rejects this paradox, since the "testimonies of Christ and the apostles" affirm that those who are justified and forgiven are also saved.

believe is condemned already, because he has not believed in the name of the only begotten Son of God" (Jn. 3:16-18 - NKJV).

It really is just that simple, and the Lutherans in the age of orthodoxy got it right. God loved the world in such a way that He gave His Son so that the whole world might be saved through Him. Whoever believes in Him is saved, justified (not condemned), and has eternal life. Whoever does not believe in Him is neither saved, nor justified, nor made an heir of eternal life.

Christ, the Throne of Grace, has made atonement for the sins of the whole world. But only the forensic appeal to the Throne of Grace justifies. In other words, faith alone justifies.

Lord, let at last Thine angels come,
To Abram's bosom bear me home,
That I may die unfearing;
And in its narrow chamber keep
My body safe in peaceful sleep
Until Thy reappearing.
And then from death awaken me
That these mine eyes with joy may see,
O Son of God, Thy glorious face,
My Savior and my Throne of Grace.[23]
Lord Jesus Christ, My prayer attend, my prayer attend,
And I will praise Thee without end.

---

23 *The Lutheran Hymnal #429*: "Fount of Grace;" Original: *Gnadenthron.*

Appendix 1: The "Causes" of Justification

Polycarp Leyser

Theological Assertions Concerning the Justification of Man before God

The efficient cause of justification is the entire Holy Trinity. For the Father justifies us, in His Son, our Lord Jesus Christ, through the Holy Spirit (1 Cor. 6).

The interior motivating cause is not any preceding merit of ours, nor any subsequent satisfaction, but only the free and infallible mercy of God, who sees the miseries of the human race, procures their redemption, and freely justifies us without any condition of the law having been fulfilled by us.

The exterior motivating or meritorious cause is the obedience, suffering, death and resurrection of Christ, the Son of God and of Man, by which He has perfectly made satisfaction to the Law for us, has made atonement for sins, has defeated death, has conquered Satan, and with the gates of Hades having been broken, has freed us for the freedom of the sons of God.

The formal cause is no inhering quality in us, nor is it the essential righteousness of God dwelling in us. But it is the remission of our sins and the righteousness of Christ alone which the heavenly Father imputes to us as our own, and by this He pronounces us to be righteous.

The instrumental cause with regard to God is the ministry of Word and Sacrament, in which God opens His heavenly treasures, hidden in the Son, and offers them to all men without discrimination or condition.

The instrumental cause with regard to us is faith, which acknowledges the fullness of the divine promise about

Christ, offered in the Word and sealed in the Sacraments; embraces it with firm assent; and rests in it with great confidence that has no doubt concerning its salvation.

And since no works of the Law, neither preceding nor present nor subsequent, constitute any cause (either of merit or of application), therefore we rightly and piously declare that *man is justified by faith alone in Christ.*

The final cause of this free justification is not only that the dignity of God's righteousness may be acknowledged, but also that our consciences, afflicted by sin in general, may have peace before God.

The effects are: adoption as sons of God, regeneration, the indwelling of God, vivification, eternal life, and innumerable other things. (*De Iustificatione Hominis,* Proposition 1, par. 4-12, translation mine.)

Aegidius Hunnius

In order that each part may be examined in order, give me such a definition of justification that embraces the sum of the whole treatment that will follow.

Justification is the act of God by which He deigns to consider the man who is frightened by the awareness of sins and who flees to the Throne of Grace with pure mercy, through and for the sake of the merit of Christ, apprehended by faith; and, having forgiven him his sins, He reckons him as righteous, free from damnation, and also an heir of eternal life, without any human merit and without any view of God toward the virtues or the works of man.

What kind of definition is this?

It is a causal definition, seeing that the true causes are being enumerated and the false causes removed.

How many causes of justification are there?

Three. First is grace, that is, the gracious favor of God.

Second: The obedience of Christ. Third: Faith.

Why do you number the causes in this order?

I put the grace of God in first place because this was given to us, as the Apostle testifies, before times of eternity, and it is also the source and beginning of the remaining causes, since it occurred by the mercy and grace of God that the Son was sent into the world to satisfy God in our place. Faith, on the other hand, since it is considered relatively to the obedience of Christ as the instrument that apprehends the thing that is apprehended, necessarily presupposes that which is apprehended, namely, the merit of Christ. In the order of causes, the merit of Christ comes before our faith, although in the case of the fathers, who lived before the Messiah was born and suffered, their faith (temporally speaking) existed prior to the suffering of the Lord, as they were naturally looking forward toward that which was to come. Still, if you consider the order of causes, the suffering of the Son comes first before God, who justifies (who views the merit of His Son outside the realm of time). Similarly, if you weigh the order of causes and effects, the suffering of Christ, is naturally prior to the salvation of the patriarchs (for this depends on the suffering of Christ as the effect brought about by the cause), although if you view the priority of time, the fathers gained that salvation before the Lord suffered—indeed, before He was born into the world. (*Articulus de iustificatione*, pp. 22-23, translation mine.)

Johann Gerhard

In this passage the causes and the object of our justification before God are expressed.

1. The chief efficient cause is the grace of God, that is, God's free favor that takes our misery into account.

2. The meritorious cause is Christ in the office of redemption which the Apostle describes with three very significant words. First, with the word ἀπολύτρωσιν, which re-

gards the spiritual captivity in Satan's kingdom, from which we have been redeemed by the precious λύτρῳ of Christ. Second, with the word ἱλαστήριον, which regards the lid of the ark of the covenant in the Old Testament. Third, with the phrase the αἷμα τοῦ χριστοῦ, which, by way of synecdoche, signifies the entire obedience of Christ, active as well as passive.

3. The instrumental cause is faith, that receiving (ληπτικόν) means that embraces the benefits of Christ offered in Word and Sacraments, those imparting (δοτικοῖς) means.

4. The formal cause is πάρεσις, the remission of sins, which is joined by an indivisible connection with the imputation of the righteousness of Christ. (Rom. 4:3).

5. The final cause with respect to God is ἔνδειξις τῆς δικαιοσύνης αὐτοῦ. In justification or the remission of sins, God remains just in that He justly punishes our sins in Christ, who received them upon Himself; and He justifies believers by means of the righteousness of Christ that has been imputed to them.

The object of justification is man the sinner, but only such a one as believes in Christ, that is, who acknowledges his sins from the Law, who seriously grieves over them, and who by faith applies to himself the promise of the remission of sins for the sake of Christ. (*Adnotationes,* Romans 3:26, translation mine.)

Appendix 2: The Lutheran Fathers on Specific Bible Passages

John 1:29

Chemnitz, HARMONY OF THE FOUR EVANGELISTS

We noted a little earlier what we must observe from the fact that he says "sin of the world." To that let me add only this: That the Baptist is showing in this way that the Messiah's kingdom was not political, for it is not like that ram and he-goat of Dan. 8:20, but a lamb that takes away the sin of the world. There is a silent antithesis in the phrase "of the world," for they used to place the sins only of the people of Israel on the Levitic sacrificial victims, but this Lamb takes away the sins of the entire world. Therefore, he is affirming that Christ's blessings have to do with not only the Jews but the entire world, and that from these blessings no one who is in this world is excluded if only they should wish to accept them by faith.

Next, Chrysostom observes eruditely that the Baptist is not saying "who will take away" or "who takes away our sins" but "who takes away" or "taking away," signifying that the continuous act or unending office of Christ is to take away our sins so long as we are in this life, and this in three ways.

First, the effective force of the expiation which took place once on the cross flourishes and is effective for ever for taking away sins, for He has found an eternal redemption. In fact, according to Rev. 13:8, it is valid from the beginning of the world.

Second, whenever we are reconciled to God, the Lamb of God is taking away our sins, not by dying again but by applying the merit of His expiation to believers through the ministry of the Word and Sacraments. Also, although sin may dwell in our flesh, nevertheless, before the judgment of God upon those who are in Christ sin is covered up by Christ's intercession and is not imputed but taken or lifted away, as Psa. 32:1 says.

Third, Christ also takes away sins in us by mortification and sanctification through the Holy Spirit which begin in this life and should increase therein but are not completed except in eternal life. Because the Baptist seems to speak principally about the expiation made on the cross when Christ bore our sins upon His body on the cross (1 Pet. 2:24), others explain the wording with this simile, as when people say that hellebore purges, they are not indicating a single act nor some specific time but signify that this is the inherent and constant power that exists in hellebore. Erasmus thinks that this "who takes away the sin of the world" was said by the same logic. Just as an herb does not heal a sick person unless he uses and applies it correctly, so the power of Christ's passion is sufficient to take away the sins of the whole world but it benefits those alone who accept this Lamb, John 1:12. Moreover, the Baptist is saying in this passage not "who remits" (something which is attributed to Christ elsewhere) but "who takes away sin." He is, after all, speaking about the office of the Mediator to the extent that He became a sacrifice for us. Sin is not remitted unless it should be taken away because of the expiation of Christ. (*The Harmony of the Four Evangelists, Vol. 1, Book 2*, 63)

Romans 3:24

Chemnitz:

(See above in the essay Chemnitz' "Common Analogy" describing the forensic justification that, he says, is "clearly described" by Paul in Romans 3.)

Hunnius:

Hence Paul, when he expressly discusses justification in Romans 3 and 4, does not know of a justification apart from faith, and especially as Galatians 2 plainly says, "Man is not justified except by faith in Jesus Christ." (*Theses Opposed to Huberianism*, Concerning Justification, Thesis 6)

Luther, Smalcald Articles:

Likewise: All have sinned and are justified (German: "werden gerecht" "become righteous") without merit [freely, and without their own works or merits] by His grace, through the redemption that is in Christ Jesus, in His blood, Rom. 3, 23f.

Now, since it is necessary to believe this, and it cannot be otherwise acquired or apprehended by any work, law, or merit, it is clear and certain that this faith alone justifies us as St. Paul says, Rom. 3, 28: For we conclude that a man is justified by faith, without the deeds of the Law. Likewise 3, 26: That He might be just, and the Justifier of him which believeth in Christ.

Romans 4:5

Hunnius

As I understand your thinking, you believe that a man who is righteous by nature is justified?

When God justifies a man, He does not justify one who is righteous by nature. For He finds none, in that all have sinned, all have become useless and unrighteous, and fall short of the glory of God. Indeed, Christ did not come for the sake of righteous people, but to save sinners, to seek and to save what was lost. Paul does not hesitate to affirm in this regard that God justifies the ungodly (Rom. 4)—not the ungodly as he continues in his ungodliness, but as he acknowledges it and turns to the Throne of Grace, Jesus Christ (Articulus de iustificatione, pp. 66-67, translation mine).

Gerhard:

With ἀσεβῆ [ungodly], the ungodly is not understood as remaining securely in his ungodliness without repentance (Prov. 17:15), but as he comes out of it through repentance and faith. This one is judged as righteous before the judgment of God through the imputed righteousness of Christ and is absolved from sins, since compensation has been made for his sins through the satisfaction of Christ. Therefore, such a penitent and believing man, who is certainly ungodly and sinful in himself, is nonetheless righteous in Christ through faith. (*Adnotationes*, Romans 4:5, translation mine.)

Romans 4:25

Paraphrase from the Apology indicating the justification of believers as the final cause of Christ's resurrection:

The adversaries approve Article III, in which we confess that there are two natures in Christ. The human nature was assumed by the Word into the unity of His person [John 1:14]. Christ suffered and died to reconcile the Father to us and was raised again to reign, to justify, and to sanctify believers according to the Apostles' Creed and the Nicene Creed. (Ap:III:52)

Luther:

Thus St. Paul declares that "Christ died for our sin and rose for our justification" [Rom. 4:25]. That is to say, in his suffering Christ makes our sin known and thus destroys it, but through his resurrection he justifies us and delivers us from all sin, if we believe this. (*Luther's Works, Vol. 42*, 12)

Chemnitz:

Rom. 4:24,25: "It was written for our sakes. It will be reckoned to us who believe in Him that raised up from the dead Jesus our Lord, who was put to death for our trespasses and raised for our justification."

You hear both things, that God imputes something to the believers, and what it is He imputes; namely, that Christ was put to death for our sins and that He was raised for our righteousness. Rom. 5:21: "Grace reigns through righteousness to eternal life through Christ Jesus our Lord." Christ is, however, our righteousness. (Jer. 23:6; 1 Cor. 1:30; Rom. 10:4)

But how can we be justified to life eternal through this foreign righteousness? I reply, as Paul says, Gal. 3:27: "As many of you as were baptized into Christ have put on Christ." At the same time we have been clothed also with His righteousness. Rom. 8:32: "With His Son God gives us all things." But Christ has a perfect fulfillment of the Law, or righteousness, for us. Therefore the Father gives that to the believers that they may be justified on account of it. 7 What I have here briefly related is the constant teaching of the prophetic and the apostolic Scripture in the Old and in the New Testament concerning the justification of man before God to life eternal. On this we should, and safely can, place our trust that we may be justified on its account, that is, that we may receive remission of sins, be absolved from the deserved sentence of damnation, be received by God into grace, be adopted as sons, and finally be received to eternal life. (*Examination, Vol. 1*, 503-504)

When, therefore, Paul wanted to explain, Rom. 4:24–25, what that righteousness is which is imputed to the believers without their own works, or what faith must apprehend that it may be imputed for righteousness, he says: To those who believe in Him who raised Jesus from the dead, who was delivered to death for our transgressions and was raised again for our justification. For that is our righteousness: (1) that the Son of God became a Mediator for us, being obedient to the Father to death; (2) that the Father accepted that satisfaction and obedience of the Son for our reconciliation and propitiation, which He showed by His resurrection. (*Examination, Vol. 1,* 529-530)

Gerhard, on Romans 4:24:

One asks, why is Christ's resurrection from the dead declared specifically to be the object of justifying faith? We reply: (1) Because by raising His Son, our bondsman, who was put to death for our sins, God made manifest by that very act that full satisfaction has been made to Him by His death. (2) Consideration is given at the same time to the power of God which He exerted in the raising of Christ (Eph. 1:20). This is how that statement is applied to the example of Abraham, whose faith is commended in 4:20 for the fact that *he gave praise to God.* (3) The summary of the entire Gospel is contained in this article of the resurrection of Christ, and this single article encompasses all the rest (1 Cor. 15:1 ff.). For it is understood from the fact that Christ rose from the dead that He truly died. And since He truly died, He was therefore also truly conceived and born, and truly suffered for our sins. (*Adnotationes,* Romans 4:24, translation mine.)

Gerhard, in a separate pamphlet on Romans 4:25, says that the resurrection of Christ provides a "clear demonstration and manifestation" that Christ....

...is the Savior; that payment for our sins has now been made and perfect redemption accomplished; and that salvation and righteousness have been prepared (see Rom. 8:34, 1 Cor. 15:17, etc.). The resurrection of Christ was indeed necessary, both on account of the clear proof and on account of the application of our justification. For if Christ had not been raised, then death would not have been conquered; rather, He would have been conquered by death. In that case, He would not have merited for us life and righteousness. And even if He had merited them, He still would not be able to confer and apply them if He had remained in death. Having stated these things briefly, there emerges this sense of the passage:

PARAPHRASE:

Christ Jesus our Lord subjected Himself to death for our sake and was delivered over to it in order that He might make satisfaction for the sins of the whole world and atone for them. He was, however, raised from the dead in order that He might testify and demonstrate that, with death now fully defeated and destroyed, righteousness and life have been provided for men; and that He might apply these things to those who believe in Him. (*Summae Evangelii, hoc est, Aphorismi Apostolici Rom. 4 v.25 Consideratio*)

(See also Appendix 4, Gerhard's "absolved us in Him")

Romans 5:18

Luther

Thus here, too, the evangelist did not intend that John or any other human being or any creature should be the light, but that there is only one light which illumines all men and that not a single human being could come upon the earth who could be illumined by anybody else. I do not know how to disagree with this interpretation; for in the same manner also St. Paul writes in Romans 5[:18]: "As through one man's sin condemnation has come over all men, so through one man's righteousness justification has come over all men." Yet not all men are justified through Christ, nevertheless he is the man through whom all justification comes. It is the same here. Even if not all men are illumined, yet this is the light from which alone all illumination comes. The evangelist has freely used this manner of speaking; he did not avoid it even though some would stumble over the fact that he speaks of all men. He thought he would take care of such offense by explaining before and after and by saying that "the darkness has not comprehended it," and that the world has never recognized him and his own have never accepted him. Such passages should have been strong enough so that nobody could say he had intended to say that all men are enlightened, but that he alone is the light which enlightens everybody and that, without him, nobody is enlightened. (*Luther's Works, Vol. 52*, 71)

Hunnius

This notwithstanding, we most willingly grant that there is a righteousness that avails before God for the entire human race, a righteousness that has been gained and acquired through Christ, so that if the whole world were to believe in Christ, then the whole world would be justified. With respect to this, Paul writes in Romans 5 that "through one man's justification (δικαίωμα), the gift has spread toward all men for justification (δικαίωσις) of life." Nevertheless, no one is justified nor does anyone obtain remission of sins from this acquired universal righteousness without the imputation of this acquired righteousness of Christ . But the imputation of righteousness does not take place except through faith. (*Theses Opposed to Huberianism*, Concerning Justification, Thesis 5)

For when it says in Romans 5, "Just as through the sin of one man, evil spread to all men for condemnation, so through the righteousness of one man, good spreads to all men for justification of life," this is clearly what Paul means, that just as through the transgression of Adam, sin spread to all those who came after him resulting in their condemnation, so through the obedience of Christ, righteousness was acquired and obtained, which is more than sufficient for all men to be justified and made alive, if the whole world were to embrace it by faith. For this is how Romans 3 explains this sentence: "The righteousness of God through faith in Jesus Christ to all and upon all those who believe." One should not look to the Huberian dogma in order to confirm the true sense of the Pauline saying. For it is true that the Apostle, in each passage, mentions the established antithesis of propagation between Adam and Christ, not only of evil for condemnation, but also of good for justification. Now, certainly if one should press each and every aspect of the antithesis, wouldn't we fall into the heresy of the papists, so that, just as sin was propagated from Adam to men through the indwelling of sin, so the righteousness of the Second Adam likewise must be transmitted and propagated to us by way of indwelling? But if we condemn this mode of propagation of the one , then it follows that no other mode exists for propagating in us the righteousness that avails before God, except for imputation. For salvation and the righteousness obtained for the whole world are apprehended through faith, so that those who believe apply that to themselves which would have been propagated through imputation by faith to all men, if all men had believed.

Therefore, although on account of a lack of faith, all men at once are by no means justified, nor were they ever justified, nevertheless the apostolic antithesis remains unshaken. Nor is the good or the benefit that is conferred on us through Christ rendered weaker than the evil that was transmitted to us by Adam's sin. For Christ surpasses Adam in this, that, since through one sin death reigned, Christ, for His part, obtained full justification from many sins for all those who believe in His name.

He also surpasses Adam in this, that Adam killed those who came after him, that is, he delivered death and condemnation to them by the propagation of sin. Christ, on the other hand, brings us back from condemnation to justification of life. Now, just as it is a much greater work to bring to life one who is by nature dead than it is to kill someone (since anyone can kill, while no one is able to bring to life except for God, with His omnipotent power), so also Christ is to be regarded as having surpassed Adam by bringing to life those whom Adam, through sin, had made subject to death.

And if Dr. Huber were teachable, the learned and vigorous response of the Wittenberg theologians could have abundantly satisfied him. This is how they respond to Huber regarding that passage championed by Huber, Romans 5: "On the contrary, isn't your conclusion manifestly overthrown by that very passage that you cite, clearly demonstrating that there is no valid reason for your opposition? To be sure, just as the condemnation pertained to all men by guilt , and nevertheless actually pertains only to the impenitent and unbelieving, so also the gift of the grace of God and the merit of Christ is certainly universal. Nevertheless, it is actually restricted to believers only—those who are released from condemnation by the benefit of Christ, who is apprehended by faith." Thus far the Wittenberg theologians.

And what will Dr. Huber reply to the Book of Concord, which, in citing these very words from Romans, explicitly confirms that those things mean nothing other than that we are justified by faith? This is what the Book of Concord says in the Latin edition, page 666: "Therefore, these statements are equivalent and clearly mean the same thing, when Paul says that we are justified by faith; or that faith is imputed to us for righteousness; and when he teaches that we are justified by the obedience of one Mediator, who is Christ; or that through the righteousness of one man, justification of life comes upon all men. For faith does not justify on account of this, that it is such a good work, or that it is such a splendid virtue, but because it apprehends and embraces the merit of Christ in the promise of the Gospel." Thus far the Book of Concord .

If the Pauline phrase (that "through the righteousness of One Man justification of life comes upon all men") clearly means the same thing as that other statement, "We are justified by faith" (as the Book of Concord clearly and emphatically asserts), then the interpretation is rejected by the sentence of the Book of Concord that imagines from these words of Paul a justification apart from faith—one that extends also to those who have never had faith and never will. Dr. Luther says it even better in [his lectures on] the second chapter to the Galatians: "Where Christ and faith are not present, there is no remission of sins, no refuge, nothing but pure imputation of sins and condemnation." (*A Clear Explanation*, 62-65)

Gerhard

This verse is a summary of everything that came before. That I may briefly summarize, he says, what I have said thus far concerning the comparison between Adam and Christ, the matter comes down to this: Just as the guilt that was contracted from one transgression of Adam sentences all men to death, so the righteousness of Christ that is imputed to believers by faith justifies them, so that they are again made participants in the eternal life that had been lost in Adam and through Adam.

ὡς δι' ἑνὸς παραπτώματος, εἰς πάντας ἀνθρώπους, εἰς κατάκριμα. *Just as through one offense*, namely, guilt came *upon all men for condemnation*. The Syriac translates: *Just as through sin, condemnation was to all the children of men*. The Apostle contrasts τὸ παράπτωμα of Adam and τὸ δικαίωμα of Christ. Likewise, he contrasts the κατάκριμα that was propagated to all from Adam's transgression with the δικαίωσιν ζωῆς that deduces its origin from the δικαιώματι of Christ and flows down to all.

Οὕτω καὶ δι' ἑνὸς δικαιώματος εἰς πάντας ἀνθρώπους, εἰς δικαίωσιν ζωῆς. *So through one Man's righteousness*, namely, the benefit overflowed *to all men for justification of life*, that is, salvific justification. For it is called "justification of life" because the goal and consequence of it is life and eternal salvation.

But how did the righteousness of Christ overflow to all men for justification, since not all men are justified? We reply: The Apostle is not talking about the application of the benefit, but about the acquisition of the benefit. If we want to descend to the application, that universality must be restricted to those who are grafted into Christ by faith. For as the unrighteousness of Adam is communicated to all those who are descended from him by carnal generation, so the righteousness of Christ is communicated to all those who are grafted into Him through faith and spiritual regeneration.

He demonstrates the basis for the preceding comparison, which consists in this, that these two men have been set up as two stocks from which righteousness and life are propagated to others. For Adam was set up in the first creation as the stock from which righteousness and life should be propagated to all his posterity. But since he turned away from God through sin, unrighteousness and death are propagated from him to all his posterity. Therefore, God out of grace took pity on the human race and opened up to us another source of righteousness and life. He sent Christ the Mediator, from whom as a stock and a tree of life, righteousness and life should be communicated to all who are grafted into Him by faith. (*Adnotationes*, on Rom. 5:18, translation mine.)

We reply:

1) The comparison between the disobedience of Adam and the obedience of Christ is not instituted simply and absolutely, but according to something in particular . For the Apostle is considering at that time the causes of our salvation and condemnation, for just as the condemnation draws its origin from Adam's disobedience, so our salvation draws its origin from Christ's obedience. Then, the Apostle considers the propagation and effects of Christ's obedience and of Adam' disobedience, for just as through the disobedience of one man, many were made sinners, so through the obedience of Christ they are made righteous.

2) But by no means is this comparison to be extended to the mode of propagation and communication, which the Apostle is obviously not treating in this passage; but he dealt with that in the preceding passages, teaching that the righteousness of Christ is imputed to us by faith, but that Adam's sin is propagated to us by carnal generation.

3) If we wanted to go beyond the limits of the Apostolic

comparison, someone could infer from the same that the righteousness of Christ is propagated to us through carnal generation, since the unrighteousness of Adam is communicated to us in that manner. Likewise, one could infer that the righteousness of Christ is propagated to all men together, without any regard for faith or unbelief, since the sin of Adam is propagated to all through carnal generation.

4) But since that is absurd, a distinction must fully be made between the acquisition and the application of the merit of Christ; or between the benefit itself and participation in the benefit. The acquisition of the merit, or the benefit itself obtained by the death of Christ is general. For as Adam, by his disobedience, enveloped all of his posterity in the guilt of sin, so Christ, who suffered and died for the sins of all, also merited and acquired righteousness for all. But this benefit is only applied to those who are grafted into Christ by faith, and only they become participants in this benefit.

5) The contrast is evident in this Apostolic text between justification and condemnation, v. 16 and v.18. But since they are contrasted under the same genre, and condemnation is, to be sure, a judicial act, from that it follows that justification is also a judicial act, and hence it consists, not in the infusion of righteousness, but in the absolution from sins. Undoubtedly, as through the sin of Adam sin is propagated to all men, for it results in condemnation for them, that is, because of it they are damned by the righteous judgment of God unless reconciliation and remission take place, so through the merit of Christ righteousness and salvation have been obtained for all, so that they may be justified by faith, that is, that they may be pronounced righteous, absolved from sins and freed from condemnation.

6) To be made righteous and to be justified are considered by the Apostle to be equivalent expressions (ἰσοδυναμοῦσι). Therefore, to be made righteous is contrasted with for condemnation in v.19; so also to be justified in v.18; and hence each has a forensic meaning. The verb

they will be made (καταστaθήσονται) indicates that these things are carried out before the tribunal of God's righteous judgment, who condemns Adam's posterity on account of sin, but absolves believers in Christ from that damnation and makes them righteous (Rom. 10:3, 2 Cor. 5:21). (*Adnotationes*, Rom. 5:19, translation mine.)

2 Corinthians 5:19

Melanchthon

2 Corinthians 5:19

...not imputing their sins to them.

This demonstrates what the effect is of the reconciliation made by the Son. For since God the Father transferred the sins of us all from us to the Son so that He might pay for us the penalty for sins and in this way reconcile again the offended Father, the eternal Father now does not impute sins to those who believe in His Son; He regards them as righteous on account of the obedience and intercession of His Son. For the righteousness of man which God regards as righteousness is that sins are remitted, are not imputed and are covered, as Paul defines righteousness in Romans 4, citing Psalm 32. Therefore, the effect of reconciliation is that sins are not imputed; instead, the faith that embraces Christ the Reconciler is imputed for righteousness.

And He placed among us, etc.

That is, He instituted the ministry of teaching about the reconciliation made through the death of the Son. For God wants it announced to the entire human race that reconciliation has been made by the Son, so that sins are not imputed to believers; instead, righteousness is imputed to them, and thus believers are saved. For this reason, among the ruins of the empires and so many sects and heresies, God has to this day wondrously preserved this ministry, and will continue to preserve it until the end of the world and the advent of

His Son, as Paul says, "You shall announce the death of the Lord until He comes." (*Annotationes Philippi Melanchthonis in Epistolam Pauli ad Rhomanos unam Et ad Corinthios duas*, 2 Cor. 5:19)

Chemnitz

Now this power of forgiving sin must not be understood to have been given to the priests in such a way that God had renounced it for Himself and had simply transferred it to the priests, with the result that in absolution it is not God Himself but the priest who remits sin. For Paul expressly distinguishes between the power and efficacy of reconciliation which belongs to God, and the ministry which was given to the apostles, so that it is God who reconciles the world to Himself (2 Cor. 5:19) and forgives sins (Is. 43:25), not however without means but in and through the ministry of Word and sacrament.

Ministers indeed are said to loose and remit sins on account of the keys, that is, because they have the ministry through which God reconciles the world to Himself and remits sins. Thus Paul says (2 Cor. 1:24) that although he has authority, he nevertheless does not lord it over their faith but is a servant and steward of the mysteries of Christ (1 Cor. 4:1), so that he who plants and he who waters is nothing, but He who gives the increase, namely God (1 Cor. 3:7). Nevertheless, he shows that the use of the ministry is useful and necessary, for, says he, we are co-workers, that is, assistants, whose labors God uses in the ministry, but where nevertheless all the efficacy belongs to Him. We are servants, says he, through whom you have believed. Likewise: "I became your father in Christ Jesus through the Gospel" (1 Cor. 4:15). Paul treats this distinction clearest of all in 2 Cor. 5:18–20. It is God who reconciles us to Himself through Christ, not counting our sins against us. To the apostles, however, He gave the ministry of reconciliation. But how so? "He entrusted to us," says Paul, "the message of reconciliation. So we are ambassadors for Christ, God making His appeal through us. We beseech you on behalf of Christ, be reconciled to God."

Thus this distinction honors God and gives Him the glory that properly belongs to Him; it also claims for the ministry the honor and authority it has according to the Word of God. For even as it is Christ who baptizes through the ministry and also imparts His body and blood, so also it is Christ who through the ministry absolves and remits sins. (*Examination, Vol. 2*, 559-560)

Appendix 3: Citations from Luther's Commentary on Galatians

Therefore the afflicted conscience has no remedy against despair and eternal death except to take hold of the promise of grace offered in Christ, that is, this righteousness of faith, this passive or Christian righteousness, which says with confidence: "I do not seek active righteousness. I ought to have and perform it; but I declare that even if I did have it and perform it, I cannot trust in it or stand up before the judgment of God on the basis of it. Thus I put myself beyond all active righteousness, all righteousness of my own or of the divine Law, and I embrace only that passive righteousness which is the righteousness of grace, mercy, and the forgiveness of sins." In other words, this is the righteousness of Christ and of the Holy Spirit, which we do not perform but receive, which we do not have but accept, when God the Father grants it to us through Jesus Christ. (*Luther's Works, Vol. 26*, 5)

If here we cannot distinguish between these two kinds of righteousness; if here by faith we do not take hold of Christ, who is sitting at the right hand of God, who is our life and our righteousness, and who makes intercession for us miserable sinners before the Father (Heb. 7:25), then we are under the Law and not under grace, and Christ is no longer a Savior. Then He is a lawgiver. Then there can be no salvation left, but sure despair and eternal death will follow. (*Luther's Works, Vol. 26*, 11)

[Paraphrasing the Apostle Paul:] "Therefore my doctrine is true, pure, sure, and divine. Nor can there be any doctrine that is different from mine, much less better. Therefore any doctrine at all that does not teach as mine does—that all men are sinners and are justified solely by faith in Christ—must be false, uncertain, evil, blasphemous, accursed, and demonic. And so are those who either teach or accept such a doctrine." (*Luther's Works, Vol. 26*, 59)

For the faith that takes hold of Christ, the Son of God, and is adorned by Him is the faith that justifies, not a faith that includes love. For if faith is to be sure and firm, it must take hold of nothing but Christ alone; and in the agony and terror of conscience it has nothing else to lean on than this pearl of great value (Matt. 13:45–46). Therefore whoever takes hold of Christ by faith, no matter how terrified by the Law and oppressed by the burden of his sins he may be, has the right to boast that he is righteous. How has he this right? By that jewel, Christ, whom he possesses by faith. (*Luther's Works, Vol. 26*, 88)

Therefore faith justifies because it takes hold of and possesses this treasure, the present Christ. But how He is present—this is beyond our thought; for there is darkness, as I have said. Where the confidence of the heart is present, therefore, there Christ is present, in that very cloud and faith. This is the formal righteousness on account of which a man is justified; it is not on account of love, as the sophists say. In short, just as the sophists say that love forms and trains faith, so we say that it is Christ who forms and trains faith or who is the form of faith. Therefore the Christ who is grasped by faith and who lives in the heart is the true Christian righteousness, on account of which God counts us righteous and grants us eternal life. Here there is no work of the Law, no love; but there is an entirely different kind of righteousness, a new world above and beyond the Law. For Christ or faith is neither the Law nor the work of the Law. (*Luther's Works, Vol. 26*, 130)

But by the true definition Christ is not a lawgiver; He is a Propitiator and a Savior. Faith takes hold of this and believes without doubting that He has performed a superabundance of works and merits of congruity and condignity. He might have made satisfaction for all the sins of the world with only one drop of His blood, but now He has made abundant satisfaction. Heb. 9:12: "With His own blood He entered once for all into the Holy Place." And Rom. 3:24–25: "Justified by His grace as a gift, through the redemption which is in Christ Jesus, whom God put forward as an expiation by His blood." Therefore it is something great to take hold, by faith, of Christ, who bears the sins of the world (John 1:29). And this faith alone is counted for righteousness (Rom. 3–4).

Here it is to be noted that these three things are joined together: faith, Christ, and acceptance or imputation. Faith takes hold of Christ and has Him present, enclosing Him as the ring encloses the gem. And whoever is found having this faith in the Christ who is grasped in the heart, him God accounts as righteous. This is the means and the merit by which we obtain the forgiveness of sins and righteousness. "Because you believe in Me," God says, "and your faith takes hold of Christ, whom I have freely given to you as your Justifier and Savior, therefore be righteous." Thus God accepts you or accounts you righteous only on account of Christ, in whom you believe. (*Luther's Works, Vol. 26*, 132)

Now acceptance or imputation is extremely necessary, first, because we are not yet purely righteous, but sin is still clinging to our flesh during this life. God cleanses this remnant of sin in our flesh. In addition, we are sometimes forsaken by the Holy Spirit, and we fall into sins, as did Peter, David, and other saints. Nevertheless, we always have recourse to this doctrine, that our sins are covered and that God does not want to hold us accountable for them (Rom. 4). This does not mean that there is no sin in us, as the sophists have taught when they said that we must go on doing good until we are no longer conscious of any sin; but sin is always present, and the godly feel it. But it is ignored and hidden in the sight of God, because Christ the Mediator stands between; because we take hold of Him by faith, all our sins are sins no longer. But where Christ and faith are not present, here there is no forgiveness of sins or hiding of sins. On the contrary, here there is the sheer imputation and condemnation of sins. Thus God wants to glorify His Son, and He Himself wants to be glorified in us through Him. (*Luther's Works, Vol. 26*, 132)

Therefore we define a Christian as follows: A Christian is not someone who has no sin or feels no sin; he is someone to whom, because of his faith in Christ, God does not impute his sin. This doctrine brings firm consolation to troubled consciences amid genuine terrors. It is not in vain, therefore, that so often and so diligently we inculcate the doctrine of the forgiveness of sins and of the imputation of righteousness for the sake of Christ, as well as the doctrine that a Christian does not have anything to do with the Law and sin, especially in a time of temptation. For to the extent that he is a Christian, he is above the Law and sin, because in his heart he has Christ, the Lord of the Law, as a ring has a gem. Therefore when the Law accuses and sin troubles, he looks to Christ; and when he has taken hold of Him by faith, he has present with him the Victor over the Law, sin, death, and the devil—the Victor whose rule over all these prevents them from harming him. (*Luther's Works, Vol. 26*, 133)

When this doctrine, which pacifies consciences, remains pure and intact, Christians are constituted as judges over all kinds of doctrine and become lords over all the laws of the entire world. Then they can freely judge that the Turk with his Koran is damned, because he does not follow the right way; that is, he does not acknowledge that he is a miserable and damned sinner, and he does not take hold of Christ by faith, for whose sake he could believe that his sins are forgiven. With similar confidence they can pronounce sentence against the pope. He is damned with all his kingdom, because he, with all his monks and universities, acts as though we came to grace through the merit of congruity and as though we were then received into heaven by the merit of condignity. Here the Christian says: "That is not the right way to justify. This is not the road to the stars. For through my works preceding grace I cannot merit grace by congruity, nor can I deserve eternal life by condignity through my merits following grace; but sin is forgiven and righteousness is imputed to him who believes in Christ. This confidence makes him a son and heir of God, who in hope possesses the promise of eternal life. Through faith in Christ, therefore, and not through the merit of congruity and of condignity, everything is granted to us—grace, peace, the forgiveness of sins, salvation, and eternal life." (*Luther's Works, Vol. 26*, 134)

By faith alone, not by faith formed by love, are we justified. We must not attribute the power of justifying to a "form" that makes a man pleasing to God; we must attribute it to faith, which takes hold of Christ the Savior Himself and possesses Him in the heart. This faith justifies without love and before love. (*Luther's Works, Vol. 26*, 137)

We are pronounced righteous solely by faith in Christ, not by the works of the Law or by love. (*Luther's Works, Vol. 26*, 137)

The question is what Christ is and what blessing He has brought us. Christ is not the Law; He is not my work or that of the Law; He is not my love or that of the Law; He is not my chastity, obedience, or poverty. But He is the Lord of life and death, the Mediator and Savior of sinners, the Redeemer of those who are under the Law. **By faith we are in Him, and He is in us** (John 6:56). (*Luther's Works, Vol. 26*, 137)

The only thing necessary is that we accept the treasure that is Christ, grasped by faith in our hearts, even though we feel that we are completely filled with sins. (*Luther's Works, Vol. 26*, 139)

By this fortunate exchange with us He took upon Himself our sinful person and granted us His innocent and victorious Person. Clothed and dressed in this, we are freed from the curse of the Law, because Christ Himself voluntarily became a curse for us, saying: "For My own Person of humanity and divinity I am blessed, and I am in need of nothing whatever. But I shall empty Myself (Phil. 2:7); I shall assume your clothing and mask; and in this I shall walk about and suffer death, in order to set you free from death." Therefore when, inside our mask, He was carrying the sin of the whole world, He was captured, He suffered, He was crucified, He died; and for us He became a curse. But because He was a divine and eternal Person, it was impossible for death to hold

Him. Therefore He arose from death on the third day, and now He lives eternally; nor can sin, death, and our mask be found in Him any longer; but there is sheer righteousness, life, and eternal blessing.

We must look at this image and take hold of it with a firm faith. He who does this has the innocence and the victory of Christ, no matter how great a sinner he is. But this cannot be grasped by loving will; it can be grasped only by reason illumined by faith. Therefore we are justified by faith alone, because faith alone grasps this victory of Christ. To the extent that you believe this, to that extent you have it. If you believe that sin, death, and the curse have been abolished, they have been abolished, because Christ conquered and overcame them in Himself; and He wants us to believe that just as in His Person there is no longer the mask of the sinner or any vestige of death, so this is no longer in our person, since He has done everything for us. (*Luther's Works, Vol. 26*, 284)

Now that Christ reigns, there is in fact no more sin, death, or curse—this we confess every day in the Apostles' Creed when we say: "I believe in the holy church." This is plainly nothing else than if we were to say: "I believe that there is no sin and no death in the church. For believers in Christ are not sinners and are not sentenced to death but are altogether holy and righteous, lords over sin and death who live eternally." But it is faith alone that discerns this, because we say: "I believe in the holy church." (*Luther's Works, Vol. 26*, 285)

But the true theology teaches that there is no more sin in the world, because Christ, on whom, according to Is. 53:6, the Father has laid the sins of the entire world, has conquered, destroyed, and killed it in His own body. Having died to sin once, He has truly been raised from the dead and will not die any more (Rom. 6:9). Therefore wherever there is faith in Christ, there sin has in fact been abolished, put to death, and buried. But where there is no faith in Christ, there sin remains. And although there are still remnants of sin in the saints because they do not believe perfectly, nevertheless these remnants are dead; for on account of faith in Christ they are not imputed. (*Luther's Works, Vol. 26*, 286)

On the other hand, Christ did not come for the smug hypocrites and the openly wicked despisers; nor did He come for the despairing, who think that there is nothing left but the terrors of the Law which they are experiencing. He was not given for such people, and He is useless to both groups. But He is useful to those who have been troubled and terrified by the Law for a time; for they do not despair amid the grave terrors caused by the Law, but they confidently draw near to Christ, the throne of grace, who has redeemed them from the curse of the Law by being made a curse for them; and here they obtain mercy and find grace. (*Luther's Works, Vol. 26*, 362)

Appendix 4: Answering Some Questions Concerning Specific Citations from the Lutheran Fathers

Luther's "the king gives you a castle" analogy

Question: Luther says, "Even he who does not believe that he is free and his sins forgiven shall also learn, in due time, how assuredly his sins were forgiven, even though he did not believe it. ...A king gives you a castle. If you do not accept it, then it is not the king's fault, nor is he guilty of a lie. But you have deceived yourself and the fault is yours. The king certainly gave it." Isn't he saying that God has already forgiven all men their sins, whether they believe it or not?

Answer: On the contrary. This statement from Luther is taken from his discourse on the power and efficacy of the Keys—the same discourse in which he says about a minister's spoken absolution: "Rely on the words of Christ and be assured that God has no other way to forgive sins than through the spoken Word, as he has commanded us." Luther is teaching that the Keys are effective, and that the spoken word of forgiveness is a valid object of faith. Indeed, the spoken Word is the only means God has of interacting with men and forgiving sins (Ap:IV:67). He says the same thing in his formula of Confession: "What is Confession?—Answer. Confession embraces two parts: the one is, that we confess our sins; the other, that we receive absolution, or forgiveness, from the confessor, as from God Himself, and in no wise doubt, but firmly believe, that our sins are **thereby** forgiven before God in heaven."

Therefore, to assert that "the king gave the castle" apart from His Word, or that the whole world has already been absolved apart from the use of the "loosing Key" is diametrically opposed to Luther's words.

> Here we have the true significance of the keys. They are an office, a power or command given by God through Christ to all of Christendom for the retaining and remitting of the sins of men. For so Christ says in Matt. 9[:6], "But that you may know that the Son of Man has authority to forgive sins," and he says to the paralytic, "arise," etc. And soon thereafter, "When the crowd saw it ... they praised God who had given such authority to men" [Matt. 9:8]. Do not allow yourself to be led astray by this Pharisaic babbling by which some deceive themselves, saying, "How can a man forgive sins when he can bestow neither grace nor the Holy Spirit?" Rely on the words of Christ and be assured that God has no other way to forgive sins than through the spoken Word, as he has commanded us. If you do not look for forgiveness through the Word, you will gape toward heaven in vain for grace, or (as they say), for a sense of inner forgiveness.
>
> But if you speak as the factious spirits and sophists do: "After all, many hear of the binding and loosing of the keys, yet it makes no impression on them and they remain unbound and without being loosed. Hence, there must exist something else beside the Word and the keys. It is the spirit, the spirit, yes, the spirit that does it!" Do you believe he is not bound who does not believe in the key which binds? Indeed, he shall learn, in due time, that his unbelief did not make the binding vain, nor did it fail in its purpose. Even he who does not believe that he is free and his sins forgiven shall also learn, in due time, how assuredly his sins were forgiven, even though he did not believe it. St. Paul says in Rom. 3[:3]: "Their faithlessness nullify the faithfulness of God." We are not talking here either about people's belief or disbelief regarding the efficacy of the keys. We realize that few believe. We are speaking of what the keys accomplish and give. He who does not accept what the keys give receives, of course, nothing. But this is not the key's fault. Many do not believe the gospel, but this does not mean that the gospel is not true or effective. A king gives you a castle.

> If you do not accept it, then it is not the king's fault, nor is he guilty of a lie. But you have deceived yourself and the fault is yours. The king certainly gave it. (*Luther's Works, Vol. 40,* 366-367)

Luther's "forgiven before our prayer" from the Large Catechism

Question: Luther says in the Large Catechism, on the Lord's Prayer, par. 88: "Therefore there is here again great need to call upon God and to pray: Dear Father, forgive us our trespasses. Not as though He did not forgive sin without and even before our prayer (for He has given us the Gospel, in which is pure forgiveness before we prayed or ever thought about it). But this is to the intent that we may recognize and accept such forgiveness." Isn't he saying that God has already forgiven all sinners?

Answer: No. Luther here is speaking about Christians who pray the Lord's Prayer, and therefore, have been baptized and incorporated into the Church through faith in Christ. He is in no way speaking about the Jews and Turks who do not pray the Lord's Prayer. He connects God's forgiveness "without and even before our prayer" to "the Gospel," "for He has given us the Gospel, in which is pure forgiveness."

Luther also says:

> The year of the release of debt is the whole time of grace, because the kingdom of Christ is nothing but the constant forgiveness of debts, so that they are forgiven. But that a debt is not forgiven to a stranger denotes that outside the church of God there is no remission of sins. For forgiveness cannot be granted to those who do not want it, who justify themselves and despise the church. Therefore repayment is to be demanded from them until they pay; that is, one must not yield to them but must always demand in order that they may think and act differently, until they repent. But to the

> repenting brother everything is to be forgiven. For where faith remains, there are no sins that are not forgivable and not to be remitted; but where unbelief remains, there are no sins that are not to be condemned and that should go unpunished. (*Luther's Works, vol. 9*, on Dt. 15:19)

And Melanchthon says in his *Loci Communes*, p.144:

> This also is certain, that outside the church, that is, among those on whom the name of God has not been invoked through Baptism and who are without the Gospel, there is no remission of sins and a share in eternal life, as among the enemies of Christ, blasphemers, Jews, Mohammedans, and the like. This is clearly proved by this statement, "There is no other name given to mankind whereby [we] must be saved," except the name of Jesus Christ [Acts 4:12].

Ambrose's "forgave to all" statement from the Apology

Question: Ambrose is cited in the Apology (Apology IV, 103-105), stating that "He forgave to all sin which no one could avoid." Is Ambrose (or Melanchthon) stating that God has already absolved and justified all sinners, whether they believe and have been baptized or not?"

Answer: No. Such an interpretation ignores the context of the whole Article IV ("The Righteousness of Faith"), as well as the immediate context, the stated conclusion of Melanchthon, and also the Scriptural context.

> Here and there among the Fathers similar testimonies are extant. For Ambrose says in his letter to a certain Irenaeus: Moreover, the world was subject to Him by the Law for the reason that, according to the command of the Law, all are indicted, and yet, by the works of the Law, no one is justified, i.e., because, by the Law, sin is perceived, but guilt is not discharged. The Law, which made all sinners, seemed to have done injury, but when the Lord Jesus Christ came, He forgave to all sin which no

one could avoid, and, by the shedding of His own blood, blotted out the handwriting which was against us. This is what he says in Rom. 5, 20: "The Law entered that the offense might abound. But where sin abounded, grace did much more abound." Because after the whole world became subject, He took away the sin of the whole world, as he [John] testified, saying John 1, 29: "Behold the Lamb of God, which taketh away the sin of the world." And on this account let no one boast of works, because no one is justified by his deeds. But he who is righteous has it given him because he was justified after the laver [of Baptism]. Faith, therefore, is that which frees through the blood of Christ, because he is blessed "whose transgression is forgiven, whose sin is covered," Ps. 32, 1. These are the words of Ambrose, which clearly favor our doctrine; he denies justification to works, and ascribes to faith that it sets us free through the blood of Christ.

Both Ambrose and the Lutheran Reformers who cite him explain where and how exactly Christ "forgave to all sin which no one could avoid." He forgave to all and continues to forgive to all "after the laver of Baptism," so that "faith is that which frees through the blood of Christ, because he is blessed whose transgression is forgiven, whose sin is covered." Here Ambrose clearly states that the "all" whose transgression is forgiven are the same "all" who have been justified through Holy Baptism and faith. Melanchthon summarizes this teaching of Ambrose in the words that follow, "He denies justification to works, and ascribes to faith that it sets us free through the blood of Christ."

The Apostle Paul speaks in exactly the same way in Romans 3:20-26, where he puts all (namely, all people) under the condemnation of the Law, but then goes on to demonstrate that "all are justified" ***who believe in Christ as the Mercy Seat*** (Throne of Grace).

Likewise, Ambrose is clearly paraphrasing Colossians 2:12-14, where the Apostle Paul locates the forgiveness of sins in Holy Baptism, which links believers to Christ's death, burial and resurrection. He is not placing our forgiveness at the time of the crucifixion, but at the time of our Baptism, which links us to the crucifixion: "Buried with him in baptism, wherein also ye are risen with him through the faith of the operation of God, who hath raised him from the dead. And you, being dead in your sins and the uncircumcision of your flesh, hath he quickened together with him, having forgiven you all trespasses; Blotting out the handwriting of ordinances that was against us, which was contrary to us, and took it out of the way, nailing it to his cross" (KJV).

Gerhard's "absolved us in Him" phrase

Question: Gerhard is often cited to prove that all sinners have already been absolved "in Christ." Did Gerhard teach that all sinners are "in Christ," and have already been absolved and justified?

Answer: Not at all. Following is Gerhard's entire section on Romans 4:25 from his commentary on Romans 1-6, from which this testimony is often cited. One should take into account his whole argument rather than focus on one phrase, as some have done. I will interject my own comments along the way.

Gerhard, *Adnotationes ad priora capita Epistolae D. Pauli ad Romanos*, the entire section on Rom. 4:25 (translation mine):

> v.25 ὃς παρεδόθη διὰ τὰ παραπτώματα ἡμῶν, καὶ ἠγέρθη διὰ τὴν δικαίωσιν ἡμῶν.
>
> The papists conclude from this passage *that our justification does not consist solely in the remission of sins, but also in inner renewal.* Pererius, disp. 10 in cap. 4 Rom. Th.

48: *Paul distinguishes in this passage between the remission of sins and justification, saying that "Christ died for our sins and rose for our justification," clearly indicating that our justification does not consist solely in the remission of sins, but that the principal part of justification is renewal of life and uprightness of mind. The resurrection of Christ was an example of this.* Bellarmine, lib. 2 de Justif. Cap. 6: *The Apostle attributes the word "justification" to the inner renewal rather than to justification, etc. For neither can it be doubted that the Apostle meant that the death of Christ was a model for the death of sins, while resurrection is a model for inner renewal and regeneration by which we walk in newness of life.*

We reply:

(1) The argument depends on this hypothesis, *that Paul does not attribute our justification to the death and resurrection of Christ for any other reason except that the death of Christ was a model for the death of sins, and the resurrection of Christ a model for inner renewal.* But the following points show that this hypothesis is false.

(2) In this same chapter the Apostle expressly teaches that our justification before God consists in the gracious imputation of the righteousness of Christ and the non-imputation, or the remission, of sins; it does not consist in our works. He cannot be stating in the conclusion of this chapter the opposite of what is deduced from the things said above.

As he does throughout his commentary, Gerhard consistently defines justification as "the gracious imputation of the righteousness of Christ/the non-imputation of sins." Both Paul and Gerhard iterate repeatedly that this imputation only takes place through faith. And as Gerhard says in the last sentence above, "**He cannot be stating in the conclusion of this chapter the opposite of what is deduced from the things said above**." But what has the Apostle been proving throughout Romans chapter 4? That "faith is imputed for righteousness."

(3) The Apostle, in this chapter, is *not yet dealing with the effects and fruits of justification*, to which renewal also pertains. Rather, he is dealing *both with the cause and merit of justification*, as is concluded from the particle διὰ, *because of*; and with the form and method of justification, which consists in the remission of sins which have been atoned for through Christ; and with the proper object of justifying faith, which is Christ, who died for our sins and was raised for our justification.

Gerhard emphasizes throughout his commentary that Christ has *merited* justification for all, but that does not mean that all have been *pronounced* righteous. Only when Christ's merit is *applied* through faith is any sinner "declared righteous" before God. Notice, too, the distinction between the remission of sins and the atonement, as well as the proper object of justifying faith. This "proper object" is not a general absolution pronounced on Easter, but Christ Himself, who died, etc.

(4) Although we do not disapprove of the goal of treating the death and resurrection of Christ as a model, when explained according to the analogy of faith, nevertheless the Apostle is not yet dealing with that in this passage, although he does later, in Chapter Six and following. Here, however, he explains the other, and indeed, the principal goal of the death and resurrection of Christ, which is the expiation of our sins and our justification before God—indeed, the merit of our righteousness and salvation.

(5) We grant that the resurrection of Christ is not only a model and a figure, but also the cause of our renewal, just as the death of Christ is not only the model of spiritual mortification, but is also the efficient cause of it (2 Cor. 4:12). But it cannot be inferred from that *that our justification formally consists in that very renewal*, because one must deal differently with different benefits, and it is proved in its place that renewal is not part of justification, but a consequence and fruit of it.

> (6) The Apostle neither in this passage nor ever, anywhere, attributes the word "justification" to renewal. Rather, he asserts that faith, which lays hold of Christ who died for our sins and was raised for our justification, is imputed to us for righteousness.

Gerhard explicitly describes, in connection with this verse, how sinners are justified. Faith...is imputed to us for righteousness.

> But if someone further inquires: *In what sense and respect, then, is our justification, which consists in the remission of sins, attributed to the resurrection of Christ?*
>
> We reply: It should be taken in this way.
>
> (1) *With respect to the manifestation*, demonstration and confirmation, because the resurrection of Christ is the clear testimony that full satisfaction has been made for our sins and that perfect righteousness has been procured. Jerome on this passage: *Christ rose in order that He might confirm righteousness to believers.* Chrysostom, hom. 9 ad Rom.: *In the resurrection it is demonstrated that Christ died, not for His own sins, but for our sins. For how could He rise again if He were a sinner? But if He was not a sinner, then He was crucified for the sake of others.*

This is Gerhard's first explanation of how "our justification" is attributed to the resurrection of Christ, based on Rom. 4:25. He emphasizes it as proof that "full satisfaction has been made" and "perfect righteousness procured." This is not a "pronouncement" that all men are righteous. This is the righteousness of Christ that would serve to justify the whole world of sinners, if the whole world of sinners would believe in Christ. It belongs to Christ alone, who distributes it in the Means of Grace and applies it through faith, so that those who are "ungodly" with respect to their own works are counted as "godly" through faith in the Righteous One. This is far different from the assertion that "all mankind has been declared righteous." In fact, Gerhard even quotes Jerome approvingly *on this passage*, saying that *Christ rose in order that He might confirm righteousness to believers.*

> (2) *With respect to the application.* If Christ had remained in death, He would not be the conqueror of death, nor could He apply to us the righteousness that was obtained at such a high price (Rom. 5:10, 8:34). But since *He rose from the dead and ascended into heaven and sat down at the right hand of God,* He thus also offers to the world, through the Word of the Gospel, the benefits obtained by His suffering and death, applies them to believers, and in this way justifies them. With respect to this application, Cardinal Toletus (in his commentary on this passage, and Suarez tom. 2, in part 3, Thom. disp. 44, p.478) acknowledges that *our justification is attributed to the resurrection of Christ,* writing thus: *Christ, by His suffering, sufficiently destroyed sin. Nevertheless, in order that we might be justified and that sin might be effectively remitted to us, it was necessary for the suffering of Christ to be applied to us through a living faith.* Christ arose, therefore, for the sake of our righteousness, that is, so that our faith might be confirmed, and in this way we might be effectively justified. The Apostle notably says that *Christ died for our sins and was raised, not for the sake of* δικαιοσύνην, which is contrasted with sins in general, but διὰ τὴν δικαίωσιν ἡμῶν, for the sake *of our justification,* which consists in absolution from sins.

This is Gerhard's second explanation of how "our justification" is attributed to the resurrection of Christ, based on Rom. 4:25. He unequivocally refers to the application of the benefits obtained by Christ to believers as the way in which we are justified. It could not be more clearly stated than that "He thus also offers to the world, through the Word of the Gospel, the benefits obtained by His suffering and death, **applies them to believers, and in this way justifies them**." The application of the righteousness obtained by Christ *is* the manner in which God justifies a person. And we are only effectively justified and sins are only effectively remitted to us when "the suffering of Christ is applied to us through a living faith." Note: he does not say "when the general justification is applied to us," but "when the suffering of Christ is applied to us." The suffering, death and resurrection of Christ + the application of the same through the Word of the Gospel, through faith = justification.

Incidentally, among the "benefits obtained" by the suffering and death of Christ, Gerhard also includes elsewhere in his Romans commentary: adoption, the remission of sins, eternal life, salvation, regeneration, and even *the giving of the Holy Spirit*. From these, it is clear that the "benefits obtained" by Christ do not refer to things that occurred or were "declared" or "pronounced" at a single point in time (i.e., either on the cross or on Easter Sunday), unless one wishes to claim that the Holy Spirit was given to all men on Easter Sunday, apart from the Word. Rather, all these benefits belong to Christ. They do not belong to all men indiscriminately. They are only distributed and applied through the Word and only received through faith, so that sinners can only be said to be declared righteous, adopted, forgiven, made alive, saved, regenerated, and given the gift of the Holy Spirit on an individual basis, "when they believe" (cf. Augsburg Confession:IV).

> (3) *With respect to the actual placement under Christ's protection from sin.* Just as the heavenly Father, *by delivering Christ into death for the sake of our sins, condemned sin in His flesh through sin* (Rom. 8:3)—that is, condemned it because it had sinned against Christ by causing death for Him, even though He was innocent, and so He withdrew from sin its legal right against believers so that it cannot condemn them any longer; or He also *condemned* it, that is, punished our sins in Christ, which were imposed on Him and imputed to Him as to a bondsman—so also, by raising Him from the dead, by that very deed He absolved Him from our sins that

> were imputed to Him, and consequently has also **absolved us in Him**, so that, in this way, the resurrection of Christ may be both the cause and the pledge and the complement of our justification. The following passages pertain to this: 1 Cor. 15:17, 2 Cor. 5:21, Eph. 2:5, Col. 2:12-13, Phil. 3:8-10, 1 Pet. 1:3.

Finally, after discussing Romans 4:25 at great length and after offering several interpretations that unequivocally refer to the remission of sins and justification of believers only, we come to the final paragraph of Gerhard's exposition of this verse, of which half of a sentence is quoted by some to assert that Gerhard "clearly" taught that "absolution has been pronounced upon all sinners."

The key question in this paragraph is whether anything in Gerhard's words supports the conclusion "that all mankind is now regarded as righteous before His divine tribunal," or that "the resurrection of Christ from the dead is the actual absolution pronounced upon all sinners." The answer is clearly revealed in Gerhard's words.

First, let it be noted again that this explanatory paragraph is the last in a series of explanations Gerhard has given. In all of them, and in all the preceding commentary, he has connected absolution with faith in Christ alone.

Secondly, even the first part of this paragraph makes clear that, in condemning sin, the Father "withdrew from sin its legal right ***against believers*** so that it cannot condemn ***them*** any longer." Gerhard clearly does not have all unbelievers in view as those who are declared free from the law.

Thirdly, in calling Christ's resurrection the "cause (*causa*) and the pledge (*pignus*) and the complement (*complementum*)" of our justification, he does not at all indicate thereby that our justification occurred simultaneously with Christ's resurrection, but that our justification is inextricably linked with the resurrection of Christ. The sense of this statement remains perfectly intact if Gerhard is referring to "our justification" as we are brought, as individuals, to faith in Christ.

Finally, that Gerhard, when he asserts that God "consequently has also absolved us in Him," is speaking only of the absolution *of believers in Christ,* and not of an "absolution pronounced upon all sinners," is proved by the supporting passages cited by Gerhard. "**The following passages pertain to this: 1 Cor. 15:17, 2 Cor. 5:21, Eph. 2:5, Col. 2:12-13, Phil. 3:8-10, 1 Pet. 1:3.**"

1 Cor. 15:17 *And if Christ is not risen, your faith is futile; you are still in your sins!* Christ told the Jews who did not believe in Him that "if you do not believe that I am He, you will die in your sins" (John 8:24). According to Scripture, all unbelievers are "still in their sins" (c.f. also Eph. 2:1). But the Apostle is here speaking to the believers in Christ in Corinth who are no longer "still in their sins," because they have been "washed... sanctified...justified in the name of the Lord Jesus and by the Spirit of our God" (1 Cor. 6:11). Yet according to the Apostle Paul, his preaching would be in vain and their faith in Christ would be useless if Christ were still dead. This indicates an inextricable link between the resurrection of Christ and justification by faith. It does not, however, indicate a simultaneous justification of all unbelievers, or of all the souls in hell, at the moment of Christ's resurrection.

2 Cor. 5:21 *For He made Him who knew no sin to be sin for us, that we might become the righteousness of God in Him.* This passage speaks of what Luther called the "blessed exchange." The sin of all men was imputed to Christ on the cross and he was punished for the sins of all men. But the exchange is not completed on the cross. Christ Himself is our righteousness, and we become the righteousness of God when we are grafted into Him by faith. We could not be grafted into a dead man, or covered in the righteousness of a dead man, or given eternal life by a dead man. Furthermore, if Christ had been left in death, then Christ Himself would not have been righteous, but a liar, and would have no righteousness to impart to anyone. Christ's resurrection is essential for our justification. But in no way can it be said that all unbelievers have already "become the righteousness of God in Christ" when Christ was raised from the dead. To be "in Christ" is to have faith in Christ. (cf. Gal. 2:16-17, Rom. 6:23, Rom. 8:1, Rom. 12:5, 1 Cor. 1:2, 1 Cor. 15:18.)

Eph. 2:5(-6) *even when we were dead in trespasses, made us alive together with Christ (by grace you have been saved), and raised us up together, and made us sit together in the heavenly places in Christ Jesus,* This passage makes it clear in what sense Gerhard meant that "we have been absolved in Christ." These verses from Ephesians are a clear reference to conversion, not to the "objective justification (or vivification)" of all men at once. In no way can one assert that "all men" have been "made alive together with Christ," "raised up together with Him," and "made to sit together in the heavenly places in Christ Jesus." This refers only to the vivification that took place for believers when the Holy Spirit brought us out of the spiritual death of unbelief into the spiritual life of faith. Paul concludes this grand section with the climactic, "For it is by grace you have been saved, through faith." In the same way in which faith links a person to Christ's death, burial, resurrection and session at God's right hand, Gerhard also asserts the link between believers and Christ's resurrection as an "absolution" from the sins that were imputed to Him. We believers have been "absolved" in Christ in the same sense in which we have been made alive together with Him and seated in the heavenly places in Him.

Col. 2:12-13 *buried with Him in baptism, in which you also were raised with Him through faith in the working of God,* *who raised Him from the dead. And you, being dead in your trespasses and the uncircumcision of your flesh, He has made alive together with Him, having forgiven you all trespasses,* It is equally clear from this passage that Gerhard connects the justification of Rom. 4:25 with our baptismal regeneration, which is entirely consistent with the Apology of the Augsburg Confession and the Formula of Concord, which consistently link "justification" with "regeneration." Gerhard connects "our being raised with Christ" and "our absolution in Christ," not to the time of Christ's resurrection, but to the time of our baptism, when we were grafted into Christ, so that His death became our death, His life became our life, and His "absolution" became ours. Since the unbaptized/unbelieving have never been grafted into Christ through Holy Baptism and faith, they cannot be said to have been raised with Him, or absolved in Him.

Phil. 3:8-10 *Yet indeed I also count all things loss for the excellence of the knowledge of Christ Jesus my Lord, for whom I have suffered the loss of all things, and count them as rubbish, that I may gain Christ and be found in Him, not having my own righteousness, which is from the law, but that which is through faith in Christ, the righteousness which is from God by faith; that I may know Him and the power of His resurrection, and the fellowship of His sufferings, being conformed to His death,* Again, the fellowship with the sufferings of Christ and with the resurrection of Christ and with the righteousness of Christ is only "through faith in Christ," according to the Apostle. Gerhard is not talking about any absolution of the unbelieving world, but of believers in Christ as they are connected to Him by faith.

1 Pet. 1:3 *Blessed be the God and Father of our Lord Jesus Christ, who according to His abundant mercy has begotten us again to a living hope through the resurrection of Jesus Christ from the dead,* This final passage cited by Gerhard as "pertaining" to what he had said about "our being absolved in Christ" is the final piece of evidence that he was not referring to an absolution of unbelievers, nor was he asserting that all unbelievers are "in Him." Peter's words are clearly addressed to believers who have been "begotten again," or "born again" through the resurrection of Jesus Christ. The resurrection of Jesus Christ is, indeed, the "cause" of our rebirth. But our rebirth was not simultaneous with the resurrection of Christ, nor can it be said that all men have been "reborn" through the resurrection of Jesus Christ. Unless Gerhard was asserting that all mankind has been objectively "reborn" or "regenerated" (which would be absurd), he was only talking about believers being "in Christ," and therefore being "absolved" in Christ.

Works Cited

Augustine of Hippo. P. Schaff (Ed.), *A Select Library of the Nicene and Post-Nicene Fathers of the Christian Church, First Series, Volume V: Saint Augustin: Anti-Pelagian Writings*. New York: Christian Literature Company, 1887.

Chemnitz, Martin. *Harmony of the Four Evangelists, Vol. 1, Book 2*. Translated by Rev. Dr. Richard J. Dinda. Malone, TX: The Center for the Study of Lutheran Orthodoxy, 2011.

Chemnitz, M., & Kramer, F. *Vol. 1 & 2: Examination of the Council of Trent* (electronic ed.). St. Louis: Concordia Publishing House, 1999.

Chemnitz, Martin. *Loci Theologici*. Translated by J.A.O. Preus. St. Louis: Concordia Publishing House, 1989.

Chemnitz, M., & Poellot, L. *Ministry, word, and sacraments: An enchiridion* (electronic ed.). St. Louis: Concordia Publishing House, 1999.

Concordia Triglotta—English, Latin, German: The Symbolical Books of the Evangelical Lutheran Church (electronic ed.). Milwaukee, WI: Northwestern Publishing House, 1996.

Gerhard, Johann. *Adnotationes ad priora capita Epistolae D. Pauli ad Romanos*. Jena: Christian von Saher, 1644.

Gerhard, Johann. *Handbook of Consolations*. Translated by Carl L. Beckwith. Eugene, OR: Wipf & Stock, 2009.

Gerhard, Johann. *Summae Evangelii, hoc est, Aphorismi Apostolici Rom. 4 v.25 Consideratio*. Wittenberg: M. Baltasar, 1635.

Huber, Samuel. *Theses, Christum Jesum esse mortuum pro peccatis omnium hominum: Contra novum horrendum, atque.* Tübingen: Stephan Gerlach, 1590.

Hunnius, Aegidius. *Theses Opposed to Huberianism.* Translated by Paul A. Rydecki. Malone, TX: Repristination Press, 2012.

Hunnius, Aegidius. *A Clear Explanation of the Controversy among the Wittenberg Theologians Concerning Regeneration and Election.* Translated by Paul A. Rydecki. Malone, TX: Repristination Press, 2013.

Hunnius, Aegidius. *Articulus de iustificatione hominis peccatoris gratuita.* Helenopolia ad Moenum, 1589.

Leyser, Polycarp. *De Iustificatione Hominis Coram Deo: Assertiones Theologicae.* Wittenberg, 1581.

Luther, Martin. *Luther's Sermons, Volume 2.* http://www.orlutheran.com/html/mlsema08.html.

Luther, Martin. *Luther's Works, vol. 9: Lectures on Deuteronomy* (J. J. Pelikan, H. C. Oswald & H. T. Lehmann, Ed.). Saint Louis: Concordia Publishing House, 1999.

Luther, Martin. *Luther's works, vol. 26*: *Lectures on Galatians, 1535, Chapters 1-4* (J. J. Pelikan, H. C. Oswald & H. T. Lehmann, Ed.). Saint Louis: Concordia Publishing House, 1999.

Luther, Martin. *Luther's works, vol. 40: Church and Ministry II* (J. J. Pelikan, H. C. Oswald & H. T. Lehmann, Ed.). Philadelphia: Fortress Press, 1999.

Luther, Martin. *Luther's works, vol. 42: Devotional Writings I* (J.

J. Pelikan, H. C. Oswald & H. T. Lehmann, Ed.). Philadelphia: Fortress Press, 1999.

Luther, Martin. *Luther's works, vol. 50: Letters III* (J. J. Pelikan, H. C. Oswald & H. T. Lehmann, Ed.). Philadelphia: Fortress Press, 1999

Luther, Martin. *Luther's works, vol. 51: Sermons I* (J. J. Pelikan, H. C. Oswald & H. T. Lehmann, Ed.). Philadelphia: Fortress Press, 1999.

Luther, Martin. *Luther's works, vol. 52: Sermons II* (J. J. Pelikan, H. C. Oswald & H. T. Lehmann, Ed.). Philadelphia: Fortress Press, 1999.

Luther, Martin. *The Bondage of the Will.* Translated by James I Packer and O.R. Johnston. Grand Rapids: Fleming H. Revell, 1994.

Melanchthon, Philip. *Annotationes Philippi Melanchthonis in Epistolam Pauli ad Rhomanos unam Et ad Corinthios duas.* Johann Schoeffer, 1523.

Melanchthon, P., & Preus, J. A. O. *Loci Communes, 1543* (electronic ed.). St. Louis: Concordia Publishing House, 1992.

The Lutheran Hymnal. St. Louis: Concordia Publishing House, 1941.

www.ingramcontent.com/pod-product-compliance
Lightning Source LLC
Chambersburg PA
CBHW071609040426
42452CB00008B/1287
* 9 7 8 1 8 9 1 4 6 9 5 4 1 *